AWAKE

María R. Mendoza

Félix A. Gómez

A

PRODUCTION

Copyright © 2012 by Félix A. Gomez and Maria R. Mendoza

All rights are reserved.

No part of this publication may be reproduced, distributed, or transmitted in any form or by any means, or stored in a database or retrieval system, without prior written permission of the authors.

FelGome Publishing L.L.C.
Middlesex, N.J.

Felgomellc@hotmail.com

TikTok@Felgomepubl

FACEBOOK@Felgomepubl

ISBN: 978-0-9886385-5-6

Printed in the United States of America

INTRODUCTION

Greetings dear readers, with all due respect:
This book has been written with the intention of enabling the reader to obtain spiritual understanding, a matter that is of convenience to everyone. At some point in life, circumstances may lead one to question the topic of spiritual sense out of curiosity.

In the following examples, we aim to illustrate as comprehensively and profitably as possible, so that you, our valued reader, through the love and teaching of Jesus, the son of God, may acquire this understanding. Maria and Felix, with all our hearts, strive to be useful and contribute our small part as baptized individuals, granted the opportunity by the Heavenly Father. We have also included, "most valuable reader," some suggestions with the sole intention of making your understanding easier.

For better comprehension, we recommend reading the book from beginning to end without skipping pages and referring to the Biblical verses located within the text. The writings in **<u>BOLD</u>** are verses collected and specified from the Holy Bible by both authors. After reading this book, we recommend delving into the scriptures of the Holy Bible. You will notice that understanding becomes much easier, keeping in mind that the Bible's Scriptures primarily focus on the spiritual.

Some information has been gathered from public sources to support the topics described in the book. Information collected for personal assertion was gather by Felix A. Gomez, guided by his faith, and subsequently reexamined and summarized in spiritual terms by Maria R. Mendoza based on the experience she obtained during death since she was renewed consciously of the physical function in communion with the spiritual.

If at any point you find the writings or paragraphs disturbing or offensive, certainly are not our intention. We urge you not to stop reading but to continue. If you are emotionally affected by the text, please feel free to contact us and share your comments. If something is not clear, avoid relying solely on your interpretation. If you require a different perspective, we recommend seeking appropriate support from your nearest Catholic Church and seeking guidance from prepared individuals like priests or attending Catechesis group services and others.

Rest assured that you are not alone; the Catholic Church is a complete and essential institution for receiving guidance and corresponding moral and spiritual assistance.

On the precautions one should consider regarding their moral and spiritual state and the suggestion to seek help: If you gain understanding and experience repentance or an awakening of the spirit, and you fear disapproval from God, it is indeed the time to turn to God by approaching the Catholic Church. Seek the help of a Catholic Priest and learn more about the sacraments instituted by the Son of God, Jesus Christ.

This Scripture would not have been published if there were no solutions. Thanks to God and the living sacrifice of Jesus, all Saints from the Old and New Testament, and the Martyrs who contributed to the renewing church's understanding of the sacraments.

This writing has been created to fulfill the duty of sharing the spiritual awakening, using specific and straightforward language with examples to facilitate its understanding.

We want to thank God for the grace He has granted us to express our spiritual identity and the opportunity to be of service according to His mercy by fulfilling our purpose. We thank you, our most valued reader, for your attention to this writing, hoping that it will be of great benefit on your life's journey toward the light—the final dwelling to which we are all entitled, thanks to Jesus Christ, the Son of God.

"All of Jesus Christ's followers were once lost, but they were sought and found in the Baptism by God. It is time for you to seek Him by following in the footsteps of Jesus Christ, a voluntary, corresponding, and constant search between two beings who love one another—God and you."

REFERENCES

*Data collector Felix, detailed and summarized by Maria.

Book's interior designs, topics, titles, texts from the Bible, organization, arrangement of initiative, and farewell; Felix and Maria.

*Book's cover design; Maria and Felix.

*Book's title; Maria and Felix.

*Book's editors; Felix and Maria.

*Warning stamp's design; Felix and Maria.

*Company's name and design; Felix and Maria.

*Translated from Spanish to English by Felix A. Gomez.

TABLE OF CONTENTS

THE ORIGINAL SIN	1
DAY THREE OF JANUARY, 2010	21
VICES OF IMPURITY	38
PURITY	41
IDOLATRY	44
THE BUDDHA SIDDHARTHA GAUTAMA	52
FAMILY CHAIN: MARIA, FELIX	64
Maria	64
Felix	68
WITCHCRAFT	71
DEMONOLOGY	74
ANTICHRIST	78
VAMPIRES	80
GANGS	83
ALL SAINT'S DAY	86
THE IMAGE OF DEATH	87
AGAINST NATURAL	90
HOMOPHOBIA	92

SODOMY	93
PROSTITUTION	94
MARY MAGDALENA	99
KING SALOMON	101
DEATH	103
THE JUDGMENT	105
BOOK OF THE DEAD	107
JESUS OF NAZARETH	109
NEW BIRTH	120
EXTREME UNCTION	126
BLOOD	129
VEGETARIANISM	134
EXAMPLES OF CHANGES OF METABOLISM IN THE BODY	138
HOMO SAPIENS	144
THE DREAM WITH THE SERPENT	147
THE DEVIL'S REVELATION	169
REASON FOR COMING TO THE USA	173
CAUSE OF MY DEATH	186
IN THE LINE OF DEATH	200

MY PURPOSE	230
Félix A. Gómez	241
Maria R. Mendoza	244
POEMS	245
The Tomb	245
Life Without God Is A Dream	246
"I"	247
The Church	248
The Desire Of My Heart	249
My Heart Seeks The Light	250
J.Soledad. Reynoso. Garza	251
In The Adolescence	252
FAREWELLS	253
Maria R. Mendoza	253
Félix A. Gómez	255
WITH COURTESY	257

THE ORIGINAL SIN

Genesis, Texts 1 through 9   **THE ORIGINAL SIN**

There are two essences: the Light, and the Darkness. The Light is God, and God separated the Darkness from Him. He called it Darkness, and far from the Light, it remains.

(Metaphor) God formed a beautiful and strong being whom He became very pleased and Called Lucifer. He was so pleased that He created many more, but to Lucifer, for being the first one, God gave him a special place, and to the others, God created them smaller in size and strength.

(Metaphor) Lucifer grew curious about what else his Creator was forming within the vastness of the universe, so he accompanied God, his Creator, everywhere. However, Lucifer, unaware that Darkness, "evil," was shadowing him, was eventually ensnared by a speck of darkness, rendering him impure. This impurity led to negative thoughts taking root within Lucifer. Contaminated and tainted by this darkness, he pondered: 'If I can seize all that the Light creates, I could assume His place and become as powerful as God, the Light.' (John 3:19-21

God longed for a place to rest and enjoy its beauty, freshness, aromas, colors, various forms of living, and pure grace. From among His creations, He chose Earth, which was then in confusion.

(Genesis 1:1-31) **The earth was a formless wasteland, and darkness covered the abyss. Then God said, "Let there be light," and there was light. God saw how good the light was. God then separated the light from the darkness. God called the light "day," and the darkness he called "night." Thus evening came, and morning followed - the first day.**

Then God said, "Let there be a dome in the middle of the waters, so that the dry land appear and God called it dry land "the earth," and the basin of the water He called it "the sea." Then God formed from the earth all the animals, the ones from the sea, the air and the land.

"Thus, Heaven, Earth, and all that is in them were completed. Then, God desired to create a special being to care for His beautiful garden, while also partaking of its bounties. This being would be so special that it would be considered His son here on Earth, fostering a bond of recognition and love between them as Father and son.

In His profound wisdom and inspiration, God contemplated, 'Let us fashion man as the guardian of all that resides here, allowing him to partake in its abundance. He shall bear My image, and all who behold him shall remember Me. Through him, mankind shall offer praise, acknowledging Me as their Father.'

Thus, God fashioned man with grace, wisdom, and love from the depths of His heart, using the elements of Earth, Water, and Wind. God breathed into man the breath of life, reflected in the radiance of his eyes, awakening him in the midst of that magnificent garden, which encompasses the entire Earth. As a condition set by God, man was to await the divine will of his Father."

God brought all the animals before the man to see what he would call them; whatever the man called each of them would be its name; and with each species came a unique dimension of lifestyle known only to them. God had transformed the Earth into a magnificent garden adorned with plants, flowers, animals, rivers, and seas, creating a wondrous paradise. Everything was wonderful.

On the seventh day, God completed His work and rested from all He had accomplished. His spirit was content with everything that had transpired during the six days of creation, and on Saturday, He returned to His dimension of light, where His children resided.

(Metaphor) Lucifer, who was observing everything with close attention, saw that everything was good until then.

The man gave names to all the cattle, all the birds of the air, and all the wild animals; but none proved to be the suitable partner for the man. And God who knew the sadness of the man's heart, **the Lord God said: "It is not good for the man to be alone. I will make a suitable partner for him." So the Lord God cast a deep sleep on the man, and while he was asleep, he took out one of his ribs and closed up its place with flesh. The Lord God then built up into a woman the rib that he had taken from the man. When he brought her to the man, the man said: "This one, at last, is bone of my bones and flesh of my flesh; this one shall be called 'woman,' for out of 'her man' this one has been taken." That is why a man leaves his father and mother and clings to his wife, and the two of them become one body. The man and his wife were both naked, yet they felt no shame.**

(Metaphor) Meanwhile, the Devil, as he would later be known, was observing everything without missing any details. Upon witnessing God's creation of man and woman, the Devil saw an opportunity to create his son, imbuing him with his spirit and dark essence (see Matthew 13:24-30 and John 8:1-58).

Once the son of darkness was formed, the Devil assigned him the command of seducing the woman, Eve, so that he would dominate the world in his descendants through her. (See Genesis 3:15).

(Later known as the Ancient Serpent, The Beast, Death, and the infamous 6,6,6; (Lucifer, Death, and the impious man,) *he sawed the weed and inherited the kingdom of darkness (on what was formerly known as Saturday day 7,) contaminating Eve in the corruption in both body and spirit. (See, 2Corinthians 11: 2-3).

The serpent asked the woman, "Did God really tell you not to eat from any of the trees in the garden?" The woman answered the serpent: "We may eat of the fruit of the trees in the garden; it is only about the fruit of the tree in the middle of the garden that God said, 'You shall not eat it or even touch it, lest you die.'" But the serpent said to the woman: "You certainly will not die! No, God knows well that the moment you eat of it your eyes will be opened and you will be like gods who know what is good and what is bad."

Then the eyes of both of them were opened, and they realized that they were naked; this is how they entered into darkness, losing consciousness of God. Darkness had seized those who were of God and for God, ensnaring them in confusion. Internally, they were dead, in a state and course of death. Darkness had entered them, bringing with it fear, sadness, and bitterness. From that moment onward, darkness inhabited their being. This occurred on the day that God had set aside for His children and His household of light – His day of rest, a day of honor and rejoicing in His creations, which we know as Saturday, the 7th day."

Suddenly, they perceived that God was coming back **and heard His present moving about in the garden at the breezy time of the day, the man and his wife hid themselves from the LORD God among the trees of the garden.** God, on realizing that they were not receiving Him, but instead they were hiding from Him, God learned of their confusion.

God called to the spirit of Adam **and asked him: "Where are you?"**

He answered, "I heard you in the garden; but I was afraid, because I was naked, so I hid myself."

Then God asked, "Who told you that you were naked", have you disobeyed me?

Adam answered: "The woman whom you gave as a companion has given me of her, and I ate."

God claimed to the woman, **"Why did you do such a thing?"**

The woman answered: "The male who hides among the trees deceived me, and I have eaten of him."

God said to the male, to the son of Lucifer: You're a serpent! **"Because you have done this, you shall be banned from all the animals and from all the wild creatures; on your belly shall you crawl, and dirt shall you eat all the days of your life. I will put enmity between you and the woman, and between your offspring and hers; He will strike at your head, while you strike at his heel."** (See, Ecclesiasticus 13:15-21, Matthew 15:13-19 and Genesis 3:3-15).

After cursing the male's body and transforming it into a reptile, God opened the depths of darkness and cast the male's corroded spirit into it. There, in the abyss, the second death, he became consumed by the darkness and rose as its embodiment, a force now set in opposition to God and His creation. He assumed rulership over the kingdom of darkness and became the father of those who are spiritually dead, entrenched in darkness, and completely separated from the presence of God.

Darkness is a realm of eternal torment where the very essence of evil inflicts everlasting agony. Here, burning passions consume the soul in excruciating flames, and an unquenchable thirst for compassion torments the spirit. Overwhelming fear prevails as God's presence remains entirely absent. It is an eternal experience of death, marked by relentless torture and a profound, all-encompassing pain that renders one incapable of crying out or screaming. This eternal torment awaits all who end up there.

"To the woman, God clarified and warned her: "Your sufferings will multiply during pregnancies, and **in pain shall you bring forth children." Yet your urge shall be for your husband, and he shall be your master."** This is Because the spirit of the serpent, "the death," will come to recognize his new offspring on the day of your child's birth. He will visit you, and you will recognize him in the pain, the pain of death.

Both man and woman come from one flesh, and they each possess a spirit. After intimacy, the woman loses inner consciousness, and after giving birth, she becomes reliant on the man's consciousness.

To the man, God warned: "For having listened to your woman," having I said to you to wait for my will, now the confusion and indignation have seized you, and you will cause effects on the Earth. Because of this, you will have struggles to obtain your nourishment, and in your confusion, you will make the Earth damn. You will fill it with ambition and plagues, freeing in its exploitation without consciousness. The plagues will be your payment, and its ruins will be the reflection of your spirit away from God that has been left clumsy and confused. "Remember, not everything is physical work; it is also spiritual".

After warning Earth, the consequences that all this will cause us, God also issued a warning in heaven.

Then the LORD God said: "See! The man has become like one of us, knowing what is good and what is bad!

God sent an angel who decreased the men's capability to live a long life in vanity and evilness. (See Deuteronomy 28:28-29). As a result, we would no longer be His children due to our inherited spiritual and corporal impurity, and thus already remaining in impurity, we would be exiled to His heredity.

Impurity acts as a veil that blinds the spirit, preventing it from recognizing God and His works. In this way, the devil came to inherit the Earth (see Ephesians 6:10-18 and 2 Corinthians 4:3-4). The animals that would have been our aid turned against all men, becoming distrustful by the unconsciousness of the man who would bring many misfortunes. For that reason, the animals distanced themselves from humans and no longer served them as they should have. Humanity was left alone, having to rely on physical and mental effort for survival.

* The concept of FREEWILL was then established for human beings, for allowing them to choose who they want as father.* (See Deuteronomy 30:19 and Ecclesiasticus 15:11-20).

Lucifer became furious over the loss of his son and subsequently sentenced humanity to suffer diseases and torments, including sadness, anger, despair, envy, passions, and pride, among others.

God's firstborn was taken from Him in this world, and the descendants of His firstborn were condemned to darkness due to the rebellion of the angel Lucifer. Despite this, God, who is infinitely merciful and full of love, sought to redeem all firstborns by setting them apart for Himself. In doing so, He also sought to reclaim the sacrifices that Cain and his descendants had denied Him.

"All firstborns belong to God, and He separates them based on the intentions inclined toward what is evil in the hearts of their parents. If these parents guide them to perdition, God saves them by taking them. This serves as a measure to raise awareness among parents for their upcoming children. If these parents have the knowledge and instruction in their hearts to nurture the soul and conscience of the new children of God, then God grants the firstborn to stay among us, to honor and serve as an example of God's love (See Exodus 13:1-2, 34:19-20, and Luke 2:23-24).

Therefore, the first son of Eve would be the carrier of darkness in his spirit and blood. Eve gave birth to Cain and then to Abel."

Abel became a keeper of flocks, and Cain a tiller of the soil.

In the course of time Cain brought an offering to the LORD from the fruit of the soil, while Abel, for his part, brought one of the best firstlings of his flock. The LORD looked with favor on Abel and his offering, but on Cain and his offering he did not. "God, who knows everything, recognized that Cain's offerings were made out of obligation, lacking sincere love for Him. In contrast, Abel offered his sacrifices with his whole being and completely pure intentions because his spirit acknowledged God. Confused and lacking understanding, Cain became disturbed and lost control.

So the LORD said to Cain: "Why are you so resentful and crestfallen? If you do well, you can hold up your head; but if not, sin is a demon lurking at the door: his urge is toward you, yet you can be his master." Man possesses the power to overcome the devil if he truly understands himself, which represents the temptation to go against God, and he has the choice between heaven and hell.

Cain said to his brother Abel, "Let us go out in the field." When they were in the field, Cain attacked his brother Abel and killed him. "Finally, the beast, (the devil) which is sin has conquered him by motivating him in fury and contempt for his brother, concluding all this in the work, separating himself by indignation before God. Condemning himself to live far away from the presence of God. Descending to the point of the crime, condemning himself and his descendants to the place where it is as if they never existed, "the darkness," getting lost in this life and the other one. (See, 1John 2:18-29, 3:1-24 and 4:1-21).

Then the LORD asked Cain, "Where is your brother Abel?" Cain answered God with lies, behaving like the son of the serpent. He justified himself in his pride because he had fully embraced disobedience, rejection, and rebellion against God at that moment. He allowed himself to be carried away by his impulses without reasoning or reflecting on the situation.

Cain answered, "I do not know. Am I my brother's keeper?" Once again, God revealed that He knows everything and that nothing is hidden from Him and made Cain see the reality of His power.

The LORD then said: "What have you done! Listen: your brother's blood cries out to me from the soil! God warned him: Therefore you shall be banned from the soil that opened its mouth to receive your brother's blood from your hand. If you till the soil, it shall no longer give you its produce. You shall become a restless wanderer on the earth." Upon understanding the power of God and realizing that he could never escape God's watchful gaze, Cain accepted his mistake and its consequences, feeling humiliated and filled with indignation.

Cain said to the LORD: "My punishment is too great to bear. Since you have now banished me from the soil, and I must avoid your presence and become a restless wanderer on the earth, anyone may kill me at sight." (See, Deuteronomy 32:10-43).

The LORD said to him. "If anyone kills Cain, Cain shall be avenged sevenfold." So the LORD put a mark on Cain, lest anyone should kill him at sight.

"Anyone who has taken a life is sentenced to a lifetime of torment due to their sin. If someone kills them, they free them from the torment they carry, passing it on to the one who committed the act (and this act of justice may not necessarily be better than the original one). The soul of the first one that killed becomes free of guilt in his conscience because they did to him the same that he did (but not in the presence of God's judgment, because of his sins). They will carry their torment until the end of their days. During their lifetime, they have the opportunity to genuinely repent through their own will and, through their actions, attempt to remedy the damage they caused, without committing further sins. If they are not punished with the same sin, they will be tormented by their own conscience, causing more anguish due to the distinction between themselves and those who refrain from committing such a significant transgression. They were weak in resisting the temptations of their body.

Since then, Cain has distanced himself from the presence of God.

Thus, God expelled Cain from the arable land, and in his conscience, he distanced himself from God's presence due to the knowledge that he had killed his brother Abel. He would wander throughout the unknown land, surviving on any food and animals he could find, progressively making himself impure.

(Metaphor) Cain would wander for a long time throughout the unknown land without humanity. Finding no other humans, he eventually returned to the place where Adam and Eve had settled and observed that their descendants had grown into a thriving village. It was then that Cain kidnap one of his halfsisters to stablish his own town.

Cain had relations with his wife, and she conceived and bore Enoch. Cain also became the founder of a city, which he named after his son Enoch. (Génesis.4:18).

(Metaphor) Therefore Cain and his children would live ignoring the presence of God and without God's illumination in their consciences. This way, they would establish a new rebellious and impure culture because they would also know what Cain, their father, did to Abel. They would feed on any kind of animals and plants, increasingly dying and becoming impure (see Leviticus 11, for impure food).

Adam was one hundred and thirty years old when he begot a son in his likeness, after his image; and he named him Seth, saying: "God has granted me more offspring in place of Abel, since Cain has killed him." "Set was only physically similar to Abel, who was like Adam.

To Seth, in turn, a son was born, and he named him Enosh (Genesis 5:6). By the spirit, he also felt the urge to invoke God, same as Abel because the spirit of Enosh loved God. And God rewards the ones that love him by keeping their offspring and renewing them. God does not forget His promises nor ignore them; He is a God, not a man.

(History of Noah, Genesis 5:28) **When men began to multiply on earth and daughters were born to them,** the angels on the Devil's side, "Lucifer," in disobedience came down to the Earth. Seeing the rebellious angels **how beautiful the daughters of man were,** the Angels took an aspect of men. **So they took for their wives as many of them as they chose.** The rebellious angels begot children to the daughters of men, and they have made that their children be praised throughout the land.

Once again, the rebellious angels acted on their whims in defiance. They dwelt among humans, teaching them the corruption of mind and body, including how to engage in falsehoods and all manner of improper acts, such as relationships between men and men, women and women, adults and children, and even repugnant acts involving animals. This led them to indulge in excessive consumption of food for mental pleasure and complacency derived from their perversions toward others. They also instilled disbelief in God, advocating for the belief in only one life, the physical one. This corruption even reached the children, as their innocence was pursued and torn.

The essence from the corruptions have risen and come to the presence of God. This plague offended God because His creation allowed themselves to be deluded, and for this reason, God shortened their days, saying: **"My spirit shall not remain in man forever, since he is but flesh. His days shall comprise one hundred and twenty years."**

When the Lord saw how great was man's wickedness on earth, and how no desire that his heart conceived was ever anything but evil, he regretted that he had made man on the earth, and his heart was grieved. So the Lord said: "I will wipe out from the earth the men whom I have created, and not only the men, but also the beasts and the creeping things and the birds

of the air, for I am sorry that I made them." But Noah found favor with the Lord. (Genesis 6:9)

(Metaphor) Noah was a correct and wise man since he was a descendant of "Set" and knew what pleases and displeases God; in this knowledge, "his wisdom," he knew that his correction made him worthy of asking God. By his wisdom, he sought to please God by converting his prayers into chants right from his spirit for God; because he knew that the breath of life is the spirit of God shared with us.

In the eyes of God the earth was corrupt and full of lawlessness. When God saw how corrupt the earth had become, since all mortals led depraved lives on earth. Because of their disobedience, God irritated set out to exterminate the rebellious Angels' children and others because of their easy inclination to evil.

God said to Noah: "I have decided to put an end to all mortals on earth; the earth is full of lawlessness because of them. So I will destroy them and all life on earth. Make yourself an ark of gopher wood"....This Noah did; he carried out all the commands that God gave him. Then the Lord said to Noah: "Go into the ark, you and your entire household, for you alone in this age have I found to be truly just." (Genesis 7:2)

(Metaphor) Noah understood that this came from God because he saw that every word he heard was true; of what his being known that it was not good as much as being afraid and staying away from such acts which could lead him to the spiritual condemnation for an offense to God. For this reason, the discernment that the destruction could happen!

The Lord wiped out every living thing on earth: man and cattle, the creeping things and the birds of the air; all were wiped out from the earth. Only Noah and those with him in the ark were left.

(Metaphor) The flood was a great signal on Earth and in heaven. Lucifer and the Rebellious Angels tried to escape into heaven, but God ordered the good angels to expel the rebels, and a big war broke out. The Devil, who by his vanity would not allow being conquered, fought against the Angels of God. God granted the power to the Angel called Miguel to defeat and to tie the rebellious Angels. God then transfigured Lucifer and his Angels in deformity according to the impurity and evilness that they had committed. A repugnant and unbearable deformation. They were all thrown into the abyss with the Ancient Serpent (Death), along with those who died in that flood. (See, Revelation 12:7-9).

God renewed the heaven and Earth: The alliance of God with men in Noah. God prohibited the rebellious Angels to possess body "corps" or to be born in them. "The Demons only have the power to torment the spirit in anger or sadness by the impurity of acceding to (Sin) for selfconviction of the person who commits it. That person is also used to making others fall into sin. As same as to give influences on others with their examples of immorality."

Noah built an altar to God and he offered upon the altar pure animals sacrifices.

When the Lord smelled the sweet odor, decided: **"Never again will I doom the earth because of man, since the desires of man's heart are evil from the start; nor will I ever again strike down all living beings, as I have done.**

God warned the interior evilness of the human beings who was free to choose his good or evil acts. God was no longer going to do judgment with the entire Earth. (See Genesis 8:22).

The sons of Noah who came out of the ark were Shem, Ham and Japheth. (Ham was the father of Canaan.) These three were the sons of Noah, and from them the whole earth was peopled.

Now Noah, a man of the soil, was the first to plant a vineyard. When he drank some of the wine, he became drunk and lay naked inside his tent. Ham, the father of Canaan, saw his

father's nakedness, and he told his two brothers outside about it. Shem and Japheth, however, took a robe, and holding it on their backs, they walked backward and covered their father's nakedness; since their faces were turned the other way, they did not see their father's nakedness.

When Noah woke up from his drunkenness and learned what his youngest son had done to him, he said: "Cursed be Canaan! The lowest of slaves shall he be to his brothers."

He also said: "Blessed be the Lord, the God of Shem! Let Canaan be his slave. May God expand Japheth, so that he dwells among the tents of Shem; and let Canaan be his slave." (Genesis 9:28)

Noah did not sense that Eve had been contaminated in her being by Evil, becoming one single person with the Devil's son, the Ancient Serpent. And same as Abel, the son of Adam who was spiritually similar to Adam; also, Cain later in the descendants of "Ham." Because of Evil, the Devil, and Death inherited the Earth.

DAY THREE OF JANUARY 2010

On January third before dawn, I had a strange dream that worried me until January twenty-fifth. I dreamed that I was in the town where I was born, in my mother and brothers' company. In the dream, the three of us, the oldest of the family, Anallely, Ever, and I, had between our arms a child, and my child was a girl. We sat on two big beds side-by-side, discussing our disappointment with our partners' abandonment, leaving us with our children and our illusions of having a happy family.

We also discussed our concerns because we were in total misery and didn't have any food to feed our children and younger brothers. In the dream, even my father had left us.

My mother said: "But God knows that there are no bad intentions in our hearts, even though we have failed in our lives, He will not abandon us and will do something to help us."

I concluded: "So everyone on their feet, and we will go outside to look in the field to see what God has for us to eat."

My brother Ever exclaimed: "Well! I hope that we still have water on the faucet because we haven't been able to pay for it".

Altogether, we walked toward the courtyard to check if we still had water in the faucet. When we opened the faucet, we began to thank God because we were overjoyed to find water.

I urged my brothers, 'Hurry! Fill up everything you can with water before they have a chance to shut it off.'

In a rush, my brothers started fetching clay pots from the kitchen and lined them up to fill them with water. As I began filling in the first one, my brother Miguel Angel alerted us, saying, 'What's that in the sky? It looks like a swirling motion moving the clouds!'

With astonishment, I looked up and asked, 'Where?' Then, I discerned a small whirlwind absorbing the sky and the clouds.

In alarm, I exclaimed: "My God! I believe that we have caused so much damage to our planet that we have opened up an abyss."

But what truly caught my attention was a small light emerging from the center, growing in size. Along with the light, there were small lightning flashes. Out of this light, an image in the form of a dove materialized, transforming into a man who seemed as innocent as a baby. His eyes emitted a radiant glow, evoking both joy and fear, as if a countless army of soldiers were present. In that moment, I recognized Him; it was Jesus, the Son of God!

I was overwhelmed with horror because I sensed that His visit held profound significance. In my heart, I whispered to myself, 'It can't be, it's You!

I was amazed to see that He gazed at me, and at that moment, I heard Him say, 'The time has come, neither a moment less nor a moment more.' He uttered a strange name, and from behind Him emerged a white spirit with the appearance of a wise and obedient young man, who, as swiftly as light, began traveling all over the world.

From where I stood, I could hear screams and cries of people in anguish, pleading for help, lamenting that death was everywhere, in their homes, temples, streets, and squares.

Terrified, I screamed: "What is happening? No, stop!"

Suddenly, He responded, 'The appointed time for the gathering of the saints has already come.

I was astonished that He knew my thoughts and exclaimed, 'But you can hear my thoughts!

He replied, 'That is how I hear them better.

"I was profoundly surprised and overwhelmed with excitement, but simultaneously, a sense of fear crept in. Yet, when I looked into His eyes, a profound tranquility and love washed over me. I couldn't help but express to Him, 'You are different from what the world had conceived of You, and so much more than what people had spoken about. If only they could know You and experience Your presence as I am right now, not a single impure thought would ever cross their minds. Out of love for Your boundless compassion and to safeguard Your purity and immense power, they would not even speak words that could offend.' 'Having met You,' I continued, 'I now comprehend what God desired for all of us. Unfortunately, we have rendered ourselves unworthy even of Your divine wrath; we do not deserve it.' He gazed at me with tenderness, as if to say, 'Now you understand.'

Hastily, I said to Him, 'I am nobody to ask You for more time in this life, but I wish I had a chance to tell my brothers about You. I don't even know if we are prepared to leave, and I'm uncertain about my brothers' purity. I can't even remember if there's anything that stains my heart. I simply hope that we can all continue together in eternity.

Still smiling at me, He continued to communicate through thought, 'You are among the last ones; there's no more time. Each one receives what is due, and my faithful servant is already fulfilling his role. In fact, I began on January first, though no one realized it until now, except for you. Hurry, you have three minutes before the angel arrives.

Admiring His response, I asked, 'What can I do with just three minutes?'

At that very moment, I saw the angel approaching, rising from among the towns and heading towards ours. His presence triggered cries of pain from those who witnessed lifeless bodies falling, even though they couldn't grasp the spiritual significance of what was happening.

With desperation, I turned toward my brothers, who were still entranced by the movement of the clouds. It became evident that they hadn't seen or heard what I had, so I urgently advised them to go to their bedrooms. I gathered my daughter and held her in my arms, while my two brothers, clearly frightened, did the same with their children. I started running toward the house, with all of them following me, filled with concern and asking why we were in such a hurry. As we entered the room, I tried to explain as quickly as possible.

Suddenly, I saw my grandpa Felipe walking through the courtyard. I barely had time to notice the Angel's touch, and he felt lifeless on the spot. My brothers were gripped by fear, and my mother began to scream and mourn the loss of her father.

I urgently exclaimed, 'It's coming for us too; that's what I was trying to tell you. Hurry, sit near the beds!' Everyone quickly found a place, except for my sister, who was the last to enter. Suddenly, the Angel reached her, and she began to fall. Then, my mother followed, and the Angel moved closer to me.

My final thoughts were, 'I've come to realize too late that the deaths of the Saints are not filled with darkness or torment. This Angel takes and guides those worthies of a holy, painless death to eternal life.

The only torment is death in darkness, in sin, and in rebellion against God. It's a pain of conscience for each of us, for not accepting our departure and realizing that we haven't done enough good. If only I had more time to do what must be done, to ensure that I come before the one true Father, for nothing is more important than the purity of the soul. If only I had more time to share all of this with the entire world so that many could find salvation.

In that very moment, I could already sense the Angel with his cold essence slowly enveloping my body. He touched my soul, and everything faded into darkness. With all the love in my heart, I clung tightly to my daughter, and with my last ounce of strength, I whispered, 'But it's already too late.'

The truth is that this dream continued to haunt me until January twenty-fifth. It wasn't just a dream; it weighed heavily on my mind. During those days, the news was filled with reports of the devastation in the country of Haiti, and discussions about their culture were met with fear and respect, particularly due to some individuals confessing to having hired Haitians for voodoo-related work. When people overheard conversations about voodoo, they would often silently withdraw.

I began to realize that this dream carried more than just a message or a reflection for my meditation. I awaited a sign that would indicate how and when to share my testimony. The dream had alerted me to this anticipation.

To this date, all my being was still shaking because the only thing in my mind was that dream. I had the patience to be sure that I wasn't mistaken; by giving myself in prayer for the true discernment so that the son of God would give me the answer. Because effectively, this time, it had led me to think that the truth about the meaning of life was not only for me to know but also for me to communicate it. I could feel it clearly without any doubt that the moment had come!

This time it was an easier way of giving me the sign. I was expecting something more complicated than what I had already experienced, like death, even though it was still very shocking to me. Until that same day when the time for me to go to work came, I thought that in that afternoon, at work, I would rest from all my worries and that I just had to wait for God's will.

Felix picked me up, and on the way to work, he did nothing else but talk to me about the same thing regarding the devastation of the country of Haiti. At work, he started talking about a lecture on the Bible. (At that time, Felix wasn't aware of what I was keeping in secret because I was waiting for when Felix and everyone else would get to know my testimony about death and all that leads to it. Also, about what Felix is, "the second witness; the witness that I entered into death," and what he represents in the book. Also, about the involuntary way of how and why I got to where he was.

Since past times, there have been countless cases of devastation of cities. Nowadays, we live resigned to something like this happening at any moment, and nobody knows more afterward; everything is uncertain. Until then, nobody was responsible for anything and was limited to only providing physical help. (We ignore the union that we should have in holy prayer).

For that reason, in consideration and coordination with the dream to share for the benefit of all, I knew that it was time to reveal the truth that Christ had granted me. Continuously throughout my life, there was an inspiration in my spirit to write a book because since childhood, it captivated me a lot, and I kept the illusion that it would be of fairy tales. Finally, today God has specified to me precisely what would satisfy my soul, on having written about the experience of death and in the way of expressing God's testimony in my personal life. And that not even my fears or illusions mattered any longer. The day has come, and it will be fulfilled. I was waiting for my physical recovery to be able to fulfill what I promised when I was in death; to deliver my purpose to God as a promise of life; I was only waiting for His signal.

I waited until the third occasion to be sure that it came from Jesus. This is the definitive occasion to rescue the saints for God before death comes to them and grabs them while asleep. The day of the awakening of souls has come, the resurrection of the dead in the spiritual world. It's time to raise the spiritual Jerusalem and expel the spiritual enemy, the one that leads us to ruin and personally accuses us before God at the time of death! We will not allow it to have any more power over us. We are alive, and we still have the opportunity! Let's tear down the veil that separates us from God so that we can get to know Him! It's time to recognize that saints are not admirable idols; they are our brothers. Let's follow their examples!

Evil is not a strange spirit that confuses us or attacks us through accidents or bad luck. Evil is closer than we believe, and we know it very well; "It is our self." As we accept things that aren't right, we start feeding evil, and at the same time, we deform our being to the degree that even our blood is no longer useful; in the Holy Bible, this is known as death. He who confronts and manages to overcome bad habits and all kinds of vices by taking control of his temptations, overcoming humiliations and the abandonment of those who wish to see him fail; "They are the resurrected ones." Those who die full of evil are those who fall into the abyss without return. They lived and died without purpose.

Many were lost in worse than just corporal death because they believed that God lives far away, perhaps in another universe! They wondered if He had already forgotten us, given that He never seemed to rescue us when we needed it. Furthermore, some even doubted the existence of the devil, as no one had ever seen him. We believe in being all alone, and so we do whatever we want under different circumstances. In my life, I came to realize that both good and evil resided within me, forming a singular identity — myself.

Throughout the generations, people have grappled with the question of which sacrifices hold merit in the eyes of God. Is it through fasting, acts of charity, or helping others that we find favor with the Divine? However, the good we do should not be seen as a sacrifice. The true sacrifice should be refraining from doing evil deeds. In doing so, the goodness within us flourishes, no longer a sacrifice, but rather a radiant expression of our purified inner selves. On the contrary, if fear or embarrassment deter us from doing good, and we begin to experience health and emotional problems, it becomes a symptom that evil is gaining strength within us.

Even though many of us may have willingly committed sins against God in the past, it's crucial that we do not continue down that path. For evil not only acts through our bodies but also ensnares us with strings of sin, one after another. It actively seeks opportunities for us to die in offense to God, thereby gaining the power to manifest as a malevolent essence that poisons others, stirring up hatred, sadness, guilt, and ultimately corrupting many souls in sin.

When faults are committed, we tend to identify with evil, and we may even come to believe that we belong to evil. We no longer feel worthy of returning to God. For that reason, due to this sense of unworthiness, we seek refuge in other people, in vices, idols, and within ourselves. We believe that if we don't ask God for anything, we don't owe Him anything. We wish to avoid judgment, not only from God but also from anyone else, because we believe we have control over our own destiny.

However, this is a misconception; we wouldn't be here if it weren't for our parents, who granted us life through their love, spanning generations. I affirm it: "that spark of life is the most-crucial because without life, there would be no body, and with life, we can even mold our body." It would be much easier to change everything around us. Nourishing ourselves with positive influences will reflect light, joy, security, wellbeing, and peace. Conversely, if we feed ourselves with negativity and evil, we will only bring heartache, humiliation, misfortune, and darkness to ourselves and those around us.

Who governs in us, the light or the darkness? Jesus was the only man who had trampled the head of temptation, not only because He knew their progeny and provenance but also because He could see when evil awakes in peoples; (He is the master at this). Evil seeks to corrupt people, making them appear unworthy in front of Jesus, through ignorance or indignation. This is precisely why Jesus loved us even more, for He understood that, at that moment, we were slaves to the evil that had resided within us since the creation of humanity.

Animals act based on survival instincts and discipline, while we don't have any need because we have more than enough talents of wisdom in a body with a wonderful mind.

The bad that we do, we do it with full awareness and even plotted. We give evil the consent to act in us by not rejecting all evil thoughts, bad but which fascinate us, and that is why we don't reject them. So, in this way, we would satiate our shameful passions, lust, vengeance, pride, and ambition, for these and other minor things which begin with a thought. We cannot help but be both fascinated and horrified by numerous dreadful cases, such as murders, violations, assaults, and so forth. It's important to recognize that by harming others, you are also inflicting harm upon your own soul.

By satisfying our low passions, we feed on evil; this signifies that the serpent lives. We disfigured ourselves even though we didn't want to realize it, initially in our spirit and subsequently in our physical being. When we become conscious of this through meditation and introspection (by analyzing our conscience), we may become frightened by our own actions. We might even seek death eagerly, by intentionally falling into vices, provoking conflicts, placing ourselves in perilous situations, or contemplating suicide.

We condemn ourselves because God leaves us until the end, up to we get tired or disgusted ourselves with so much impurity. He does not condemn us; (if we turn away from God, we fall into the desires of our hearts). We fall into temptation; we experience evil which then would drag us to indignation. It is necessary to recognize God's goodness, peace, and harmony, which only in Him is found. It is apt to us to decide for ourselves whom do we want to govern in our body, light, or darkness.

I believe in prayers because they allow our good spirit to lament and clamor to God for strength. Through prayer, we can confess the wrongs we have committed, feeling the pain of repentance in our hearts, both for the harm we have caused others and ourselves. On that day when the spirit confesses to God, saying, "Yes, I did it, I am guilty. I committed something horrible, shameful, and dirty because I was a coward and didn't reject evil when it pursued me! In moments of anger, I allowed the serpent to become the dragon that ruined everything, even my conscience. I hated my peace, my love for others and myself, and I rejected my place in eternity and society." On that day, when we confess before God what remains of us, a prisoner of evil. On that day, look for God with avidity, you will be free by the love of God, and you will know it.

I believe that in the spiritual liberation, which is to break the chain of sins, Jesus did miraculous healing in His time; He instructed in the spirituals. "He who profanes his body destroys himself." But if one repents out of love for God, Jesus then segregates them, if they could bear the pain and anguish of their illness, spiritual, mental, and body without despair, offering everything to God up to the end. That's where the initiation begins for God to raise one more being; dead in the wisdom of man, evilness; like being reborn into the understanding of God's love!

We should love God alone because anyone who is not with God is against Him. If a single person with God can inspire such fear and respect for generations, like the ancient prophets, then one can only imagine the incredible and marvelous possibilities if there were an entire nation of God's people.

In theory, God liberated His people from the people of Ancient Egypt, not from those who enslaved them, but from what enslaved them spiritually in this world. This enslavement stemmed from debauchery resulting from the perturbation and misperception that men and women obtain through the consumption of alcohol, drugs, and the worship of idols, not only objects but also people and others (see Exodus 20:1-26).

Another form of idolatry hidden under the name of love is exemplified by the belief that, for love, anything goes. This can manifest as practices like witchcraft or conceiving children to entrap someone, where these innocent children are used without mutual consent. Other manifestations include disfigurement of the body, rape, physical and moral abuses, murders for love, falling into sadness due to intoxication or drunkenness, even going as far as committing suicide, and succumbing to madness due to heartbreak. Additionally, there's transsexualism in men and women, which represents a complete distortion of the spiritual being, the mind, and the body. Those who feel unsuccessful seek a change of life and body in the hope that it will improve their situation, but this only leads to living outside of reality, ultimately resulting in ruin.

There is joy and energy when we are young, but when this phase ends, the party ends, and we are left to collect what remains. But if there is nothing left, then what is the meaning of life or existence? The worst thing is that we often fail to prepare ourselves for the last day of our lives, to provide justification for our mistakes to those who will remain, and not with another life, would be enough for us to amend them. We are left with our consciences tormented, knowing that we came to this life only to cause misfortunes.

We squandered our time on things that held no value. We also neglected our talents and special gifts, which are given to us as proof of the only true love, that from God our Father. We have inherited these talents from before birth so that when we reach our final day, our consciousness will reveal whether we squandered them or multiplied them. This is what we will present as an offering to God so that through our works, we will be recognized as His children and thereby enter the Kingdom of Our Father, God.

God provides everything for us to find happiness in our talents, but we often prefer what holds no meaning, causing harm not only to ourselves but also to others. We lose sight of ourselves, and, in doing so, we become influences on others, leading them astray. God desires to save us from this perdition and to liberate our spirits, which dwell in darkness, away from God's light. We must also nourish our spirits through prayer.

VICES OF IMPURITY

Impurity traps and entertains men and women in this world. Making them lose consciousness that a spirit from God lives in their body—a body that has been given to us as a precious gift from God. It is a body in which we can enjoy the colors, shapes, scents, the sense of touch, and more. This gift gives us the privilege of sharing the love of God with our partner, our children, and of having respect for others and ourselves through pure and godly love. It also grants us the privilege of seeing God's creations in the wonders of this world.

When one falls into sin, the sin of selfpleasing and the desire for only the things of this world, such as fame, power, and physical pleasures like sex, alcohol, drugs, and others, one automatically loses the spiritual aspect. One has freely renounced the right to heaven and ends up trapped in a rampage over which one loses control. It is a state where one has one foot on earth and the other in hell.

He who consents to evil and then intends to resign from it realizes too late that he had to pay with the most valuable things he possessed, such as his reputation, dignity, youth, health, family, and more. Renouncing evil is not easy because the devil and his accomplices have no compassion, especially for those who want to break free from it. The temptations will always be present, and above all, they must be overcome. The people who are being manipulated and working for the devil would not allow someone to denounce and give testimony to all the horrible things they have carried out. These accomplices always yearn for power over those who don't know evil, so that these innocent people would admire and praise them as wise or heroes, even though they are not, as they appear at their convenience, not when needed.

Who has died and returned to ensure that there is no heaven or hell? He who has had an experience with death knows well that things of this world will remain here, but spirits are eternal, regardless of where they end up, whether in heaven or hell. For example, if someone's spirit was destined for hell, I don't think they would want to stay there eternally or see others fall into it. On the contrary, whoever becomes familiar with heaven would like to depart immediately and take everyone else with them to share it for eternity. Therefore, we shouldn't do evil! Unfortunately, anyone in hell can no longer come out; it is eternal punishment!

The evil we commit is because impurity confounds us, and the desire for worldly things compels us to torment ourselves and even commit foolish acts due to our lack of knowledge of God and the help of the demons who have been working since the beginning of humanity. The demons learn of our heart's desires and facilitate our ruin, making it more difficult for our inner struggle to rescue our spirit.

It takes courage to be willing to fight every day for something that is priceless, which is "The Glory of God." Because, at the time of death, nothing material that we possess will be of any benefit to us. There is no corruption there; the only things of worth are our works according to our intentions.

Impurity makes us unconscious because it turns us against God, making us please ourselves in things contrary to God. But God is so merciful that He lets us know about the things that displease Him; they are written in the Holy Bible, so that we may align ourselves with His will.

.

PURITY

Purity: the benefits and knowing how to distinguish it. How to recognize that you are with God; God is in the peace, in the tranquility of the conscience of knowng that we haven't committed works against Him and our brothers because they also possess a spirit like us. Purity for us is a sign of alliances with God, and as a result, we achieve harmony in our spirit, mind, and body.

Only in God can we acquire what is priceless, which is inner peace. In Him, there is no corruption or bribery. We obtain it by our efforts, making us pleasant in everything, by sacrificing not to access things that are dangerous to the spirit, which are the desires of the flesh.

The flesh is of the mortal world, and while its time elapses, it lives aware of the pleasures it can acquire because it recognizes that its time is short. Likewise, the mind also wants to live, showing its creative ingenuity, "but peace belongs to the spirit and for him to live".

All sorts of foods that are digested cause effects in our body and alter or stimulate the mind, and if there is constant or excessive consumption of certain foods, these could cause addiction known as bad habits. Our mind by not having them causes an effect of threats to become ill, desperation, and (anxiety) for obtaining them.

Consuming a significant amount of food without any nutrient benefits harms, weakens, and affects the nervous system by excess weight. It causes damage because of mental efforts and, of course, also causes effects in our character which affects our relationship with others. Our character suffers physical alteration, excess fat, and muscle damage since they must move from its place to give space to the fat. This physical alteration causes nerve damage which affects the brain (what they call arthritis) by poor diet or bodily expansion. And other consequences such as heart attacks, through the effort of blood circulation and insufficient oxygen, leading to death after having lived a life with many emotional and physical problems.

God made us in His image, and as proof of His love for us, He gives Himself to us. He shows Himself to us in the food that He offers us in each season. The earth itself produces fruits and vegetables for our physical, mental, and spiritual health, seasoned and complete when combined with gratitude to God. He gives us understanding with this revelation; His constants approach towards us by His infinite love (He never abandons us.) God gives us life and gives it to us in many ways because He wants us to live in body and spirit.

"The flesh attracts the flesh, to the things of the flesh and for the flesh;" this means that if the temptation of food is uncontrollable and corporal gain shows, it will cause the desire for impure things (weaknesses, anxiety) for alcohol, drugs, sex, anger, personal dissatisfaction, sadness and among others. And the desire to possess more, and more material things will lead to more concerns, diseases, crimes, among other acts. These are all symptoms that can ultimately result in spiritual death. We distance ourselves from healthy things and a fulfilling life in gratitude to God as we gradually move away from Him. (For meditation, see Leviticus 11).

IDOLATRY

(Isaiah 44: 6-20)

All whose make idols are nothing, and the things they treasure are worthless. Those who would speak up for them are blind; they are ignorant, to their own shame. Who shapes a god and casts an idol, which can profit nothing? People who do that will be put to shame; such craftsmen are only human beings. Let them all come together and take their stand; they will be brought down to terror and shame.

The blacksmith takes a tool and works with it in the coals; he shapes an idol with hammers, he forges it with the might of his arm. He gets hungry and loses his strength; he drinks no water and grows faint. The carpenter measures with a line and makes an outline with a marker; he roughs it out with chisels and marks it with compasses. He shapes it in human form, human form in all its glory, that it may dwell in a shrine. He cut down cedars, or perhaps took a cypress or oak. He let it grow among the trees of the forest, or planted a pine, and the rain made it grow. It is used as fuel for burning; some of it he takes and warms himself, he kindles a fire and bakes bread. But he also fashions a god and worships it; he makesan idol and bows down to it. Half of the wood he burns in the fire; over it he prepares his meal, he roasts his meat and eats his fill. He also warms himself and says, "Ah! I am warm; I see the fire." From the rest he makes a god, his idol; he bows down to it and worships. He prays to it and says, "Save me! You are my god!"

They know nothing, they understand nothing; their eyes are plastered over so they cannot see, and their minds closed so they cannot understand. No one stops to think, no one has the knowledge or understanding to say, "Half of it I used for fuel; I even baked bread over its coals, I roasted meat and I ate. Shall I make a detestable thing from what is left? Shall I bow down to a block of wood?"

Such a person feeds on ashes; a deluded heart misleads him; he cannot save himself, or say, "Is not this thing in my right hand a lie?" (Also see; Romans 1:25-32, 1Corinthians 8:1-13, 10:1-33, kings 15:9-13, Jeremiah 10:1-16, Daniel 14:1-22, 4:5-20 Baruch 6:1-71, Wisdom 13, 14, 15 and Isaiah 66:1-6).

The day of my judgment has come, and the time to present my mission. When I was asked about my achievements, I saw myself empty-handed. I rose in spirit to search throughout the universe, searching desperately for a way to save my soul. I saw three quarters of the Earth's population kneeling, offering up to their children's bread as tributes to statues of deformed idols. Their lives and those of their generations were enslaved to serve useless Idols, images where nothing dwells, neither good nor evil.

In spirit, I asked God: "But they are all united worshiping something that also came out of your creation, so they are worshiping you anyway; what is wrong about this?"

God said: "For worshiping idols, they turn their back at me. Their sacrifices and lives are offered to this abomination when I had created them, hoping to please myself with them, as a parent pleases himself from the hugs and kisses of his children."

"But, Lord, you are God. You can change all this!"

He answered: "I have left them so that when ruin, plagues, and misfortunes come to them, they would call upon their idols and see that these don't save, don't rise or move because there is no life in them. And thus, those who worship these images may reconsider and return to me, who gives them life and everything in it. However, they can't; they have taken refuge in this, their god, to fulfill their impure heart's desires. Don't they realize that all this can only come from evil! Of this, the demons delight themselves. They confuse them so that those who worship them will be lost.

The images, the idols, "belong to the demons." (See, Matthew 15:7-20).

At that moment, I understood that death had dominion. It was governing these threequarters of the Earth because if the world ended at any given time, all these people would be heading into darkness. God would lose all of them, would lose all these children forever!

I also understood that, nevertheless, God loves us; He is patient with us and yet does not take our lives but instead extends it to give us time so that the conversion through reflection would come to us.

"He who won't kneel before the beast, the beast would kill him, but he who kneels has already lost his life."

If anyone worships the beast "death" or to its image and consents to be marked, they will have to drink from the cup of pure anger of God; will fall into all kinds of disturbances here on Earth. In the plagues is where the wrath of God is fulfilled so that we would reflect. He who does not meditate to come out of this state of suggestion, ignorance, practice, or perturbation will be lost and tormented with fire and brimstone in front of God, Jesus, and all Saints on his judgment day.

From the cup of the wrath of God, the Saints will also drink to be tested. This is the time of ordeal for all those who keep the commandments of God and faith in Jesus. These ordeals or temptations are not only for some and not others; they are for all humanity. In the ordeals it is where the perfection of the soul or spirit lies. It is not just about enduring but rather about exclaiming out to God to understand and recognize the error so that with God's help, we can escape in time.

With understanding, the spirit is liberated from the ties such as hatred, sorrows, and resentments that come from evil, which blind us and prevent us from seeing the glory that God has for us. Doubts about the existence of God arise, and we lose faith in Him!

To those who prove victorious in the ordeal, it means they have achieved Holiness or awakened to consciousness of life and death, with full awareness of their gifts and talents, as well as an understanding of respecting their limitations and those of others. The ordeal must be passed to attain holiness. The reward of holiness frees you from the impurity of the world, from the second death of spiritual state, and makes you a participant in the eternal light of eternal life.

No one deceives God. He knows the most intimate aspects of our being. To enter His Kingdom, it is necessary to inscribe ourselves in the book of life where His calls to the spiritual House are enrolled (through Baptism). Since He has also shown me the hearts of a few men saved in their spirits in pleasant purity to God and are also heard by God, pleased by God in everything they ask; these are (The Priests), who serve as intermediaries between God and humanity.

This third part of idol worshipers did not even have the possibility of changing. Because as soon as they learned of God's commandments, they would enclose themselves in their own hearts, preferring not to know anything about the One True God.

I also saw another kind of idolater; they would make idols of their own bodies. They would go to great lengths to deform and please their bodies. They were capable of stealing, cheating, engaging in prostitution, and believing they were doing something good to improve their bodies. They subjected their bodies to exercises, drugs, and even cosmetic surgeries like implants and tattoos.

God, in a moment, showed me the bodies formed of these individuals, but He also made me feel and understand for a moment how all this affected their brain. Their brains were submitted to withstand a large amount of pain, and the brain endeavored to make the pain disappear. As a result, the brain's normal function became unbalanced, leading to the distribution of incorrect information to the body, manifesting in diseases to alleviate the torment and pain.

Others made idols of their partners. They would submit themselves to anything, even if it was harmful, all in the name of love, often forgetting about God. For their partners, they were capable of hatred, crimes, murder, suicide, and other destructive acts.

Those who have excessive selfesteem made idols of themselves, and the devil took advantage of their desires, leading them away from God. The devil presented thousands of forms of temporary pleasures, confusing and using them to lead others astray.

It is easier for demons to defeat those who possess ambitious hearts, leading them into vices and ruin. They become envious of those who have stayed away from evil. Instead of seeking God, they distance themselves further, allowing themselves to be used as puppets by evil, even leading to cases of transsexuality. All this is a consequence of the desires stored in their hearts, leading to evil thoughts and actions, symptoms of a very materialistic nature.

Another form of idolatry is to admire another person and wanting to be that person, losing sight of the unique being that God has provided us with. We are unique, with our limitations, virtues, gifted, and talented. God sees what we keep hidden in the deepest part of our hearts and spirits, and our purity determines how pleasing we are to God.

"The cross" is the responsibility that God has given us. It is our identity as male or female. Be content with who you are, be pleasing before God, without deception, and without pretending to be something you are not.

THE BUDDHA SIDDHARTHA GAUTAMA

Around the 5th century BC, Siddhartha Gautama founded Buddhism; Apparently, in this story, various episodes of crisis were discovered, which serve as keys and contribute to the spiritual quest of human beings. The Buddha, as he would later be known, was someone who had compassion and had suffered through observing different life situations, as depicted in the history of his life.

Despite his father's precautions, he managed to leave the palace on four occasions. During these encounters, he witnessed, for the first time in his life, an old man, a sick man, a corpse, and finally, a monk. A monk, in this context, refers to a person engaged in the practice and pursuit of spiritual perfection, leading a simple and sober life, known at that time as an ascetic. These were realities he had never personally encountered.

At the age of 29, after contemplating these four encounters, Siddhartha decided to embark on a personal quest to investigate the problem of suffering. This decision is known as the "great renunciation," wherein he renounced all his assets, inheritance, and social position to pursue religious and holy practices.

Siddhartha realized, after nearly dying of hunger due to strict fasting, that moderation between the extremes of mortification and indulgence could increase his energy, clarity, and meditation. He referred to this discovery as the "middle way." After making this discovery, he ate something and sat under a fig tree, vowing not to rise until he found a solution to suffering (See Daniel 10:2-12 and Matthew 4:1-2).

During the first part of the night, he gained knowledge of his previous existence, (discovered the lifestyle in which he had lived before). In the second part of the night, he learned to see beings die and be reborn according to the nature of their actions, (in the good or evil). Finally, during the last part of the night, he purified his mind and directly understood the Four Noble Truths.

As a final test arose "Mara," interpreted as a daemon, which is the temptation or the invitation to evil in the people's ambitions, which made him a series of temptations. However, Siddhartha did not succumb to these temptations. With what he managed to be free from clinging to passions but without repression of these, thereby destroying the fourth and fifth chain. (See Matthew 4:3-11 and Exodus 20:3-6).

In the end, he knew that he had achieved a final state which he called the "cessation of suffering." He stated, "What needed to be done is done."

After attaining enlightenment, he devoted his life to spreading his discoveries in the northern of India (See Luke 4:14-37).

"All human beings have the potential to achieve the cessation of suffering and comprehension of nature, which is the awakening." (See 1Corinthians 15:29-58).

The purpose of Buddhism is the definitive elimination of suffering, dissatisfaction with life, or the discontents that inevitably manifest at one time or another in life. The cause of dissatisfaction, frustration, stress, etc., is the desire which is understood as the movements of the will for acceptance or rejection, leading to clinging, resentment, concern, fear, and other emotions (See, Galatians 5:13-26 and 6:1-16).

These passions are developed by an "ego" that is experienced as entirely and exclusively existing. It suffers and believes it depends on various material or emotional factors to exist. In Buddhism, this is considered an illusion to which individuals cling. Therefore, it is an effect that arises from ignorance, which is a wrong, erroneous perception of life (See Romans 7:14-25 and 8:1-21).

According to Buddhism, the definite cessation of this problem occurs after awakening. This awakening is the cessation of an erroneous perspective on the environment in which one lives and the life they lead. The person directly realizes the true nature of reality and themselves. Awakening consists of a direct experience beyond physical understanding and the objects and wonders of reality, including the person, which were previously experienced unrealistically. "The result is that the person becomes aware of the existence of a Creator, who is God."

This transformational experience leads to a new, incomprehensible state that can only be illustrated through examples. It instructs the follower on how to achieve it, aiming to prevent extremes of excessive satisfactionseeking on one hand and unnecessary suffering or mortification on the other. This spiritual awakening leads to the understanding of wisdom, ethical conduct, and the training or cultivation of the mind and heart through concentration, attention, and full consciousness of the present moment continuously.

The liberation of the individual does not rely solely on analytical, theoretical, or intellectual knowledge, but on its genuine understanding and internal acceptance, considering its capabilities and limitations, good intentions, and actions for the spirit.

Every intentional action produces one or more effects, whether through speech, physical actions, or thoughts (intentional or reflexive acts). Any movement of the will is of the spirit, even though it is not physically conscious.

The distinction between a good or bad spirit depends on the underlying intentions of actions, determining differences in the length of life, wealth, beauty, health, or wisdom among beings. In reality, these outcomes do not occur by coincidence but are influenced by the spirit. A person's role in spiritual actions is expressed through their individuality and the experience of personal awakening.

Mental factors stemming from various combinations (including the Holy Bible, television, radio, readings, and other influences) give rise to potential states of consciousness and physical changes influenced by one's will. In this case, the movements of the will exist, and it is where habits and tendencies are determined or reinforced. The differences of actions are only expressed in terms of ability or skill. They are awkward for being wrong and skillful for being healthy with good intentions.

In a cycle of suffering, some people are trapped by ignorance. As long as ignorance is not eradicated, this process will continue endlessly and be passed on from one generation to another. The cycle repeats itself without an end in sight.

"Seeking to eradicate ignorance and the breaking of this chain, the cessation of this cycle?" (See Ephesians 5:8-20).

The Renaissance or awakening: the process will force the existence of conscious beings to manifest itself. The Renaissance is not seen as something desirable; it enables the person to eliminate this chain of cause and effect. Until there does not exist a cessation of this cycle, our life is samsara (pagan).

Each individual must experience all the circumstances in which they find themselves. Simultaneously, they are responsible for their decisions in response to these circumstances. There is no owner of their thoughts, (someone who can manage thoughts), but each individual is solely responsible for how they choose to act upon them. Acceptance or rejection is, therefore, the key to achieving more balance and respect for oneself and the world—an awakening, an enlightenment (See Matthew 13:37-43 and Ephesians 6:10-18).

The Buddha Gautama affirmed that the cessation of suffering and exiting the circle is possible by locating the origin and getting to the detachment of (resentments, ambitions, hatreds, sorrows, and addictions) which is revealed as you progress through the process of rebirth or awakening. Therefore, achieving this state of liberation involves living a new experience on the nature of life, death, and the world that surrounds us.

Duhkha: "referred to the suffering exists", the cause; desire, lust, ambition, and anxiety. The root of Duhka is the lust and the anxiousness or the thirst for pleasant conditions or situations. We mistakenly believe that any act, achievement, object, person, or environment will take us to the permanent satisfaction of the "ego." However, this is nothing more than a fleeting fabrication in the mind, giving rice to a longing that is the illusion or ignorance within the cycle of samsara life (pagan). Samsara beings fail to grasp the true nature of how the spirit operates (See Colossians 3:5-17).

There is a noble way to achieve this cessation; the discipline to eliminate ignorance and pursue the desire for wisdom, ethics, and meditation. Wisdom: vision or proper comprehension, correct thought or intention. Ethical conduct entails correct speech, correct action, and correct way of life. Mental discipline encompasses meditative effort, mindfulness of the present moment, correct meditation or concentration, and the practice of nonharming, nonrestraint, and nonattachment; this path is known as the middle way.

Any action could have a harmful or detrimental consequence to oneself or others. The expression of a skillful mind is one that avoids all actions likely to cause suffering or remorse. Both the effort and the intention will determine the final action.

"Meditation's purpose is to cultivate the mind. It is a deliberate practice that helps participants ground themselves in reality, leading to increased comprehension, wisdom, mental calmness, peace of mind, and inner peace.

"As the biblical passage in 2 Corinthians 4:1-18 and 5:1-10 reminds us, **"We have this treasure in jars of clay."**

In Buddhism, the lotus is the symbol of awakening. The blossoming of the lotus represents the moment of the holiness of the spiritual awakening.

The Buddha only reached the perception of the spirit dwelling within a body. This spirit is aware, but the body is not. The body serves as a means to access the material world. For this reason, we serve ourselves of both the visible, like water, and the invisible, such as oxygen. We can see water but not oxygen. The Buddha only got to the line between life and death; he managed to see what was out of the material things. It is like the dimension of form and essence. After experiencing everything that exists beyond the material world and remaining corporeal, this experience is known in the expression of the "Renaissance"; because there is the risk that the beings existing in this spiritual dimension might conquer the spirit of the person, preventing them from returning to corporal life.

The spirit cannot possess a body that is not its own. The body and the spirit are perfectly compatible in essence.

The Buddha understood that one could not live in all matter or all essence; a balance is needed. To achieve this balance, one relies on the power of conscience, engages in reflective analysis and meditation on what is good and bad. Through this process, one arrives at a firm decision regarding their desires, choosing either evil in darkness or gleaming in joy.

Renaissance: There are hardly any people who look for it. Most people fear this by being unknown to them, and they prefer not to leave what they already know. In fact, they feel very comfortable with their current life and even enjoy it. The Buddha referred to this as 'samsara life,' "while Catholicism called it 'Paganism."

Living this new spiritual awakening life requires an ongoing process of dispossession and nonattachment to material possessions while still owning goods, and not grasping for feelings of hatred, sadness, or passion, without ceasing to be social and affectionate. It also entails having the capacity for detachment without losing respect for yourself or others.

Regarding this, the Buddha emphasizes the cultivation of the mind. He tries to express that through meditation, we clean our thoughts, discarding those that harm our way of life and using those which will make us better as people or those which will lead us to the advantages of bettering ourselves.

The Buddha did not enter death; he didn't speak of heaven or hell. He didn't encounter death because he didn't go through agony. He speaks of a Renaissance, "spiritual awakening" but he remains the same person, although he does highlight demons or what he calls "Mara," aberrant beings offering him ambitious temptations to evil. Furthermore, he doesn't give testimony of a God since he didn't enter judgment.

The Buddha: "A man who reached the "awakening," which is to become aware that a spirit exists in each one of us. And that overwhelmed thoughts can be controlled by us by becoming aware that they are part of being alive in the body as well as all other sensations. The difference is that not everything is good, and individuals must make a definitive choice.

In the Catholic Church, this is considered to have achieved "Holiness" through the faith that there is another life after this one or through the extraordinary experience of the agony, death, judgment, and having the privilege of returning to this life with all its advantages and disadvantages.

We shouldn't worship any image in particular or make requests; rather, we should follow the example of those who have become aware of the existence of God, like The Saints. Since absolutely nothing or nobody has the power to condemn or save a soul. Only he who can give us a trial, that being that knows all our weaknesses and all our works in good or evil because he also possesses a body like us, "He is the Son of God, our Lord Jesus Christ"!

In the same way, as it is designated a day of all saints for recognition whether they are known or unknown; "The Buddha was designated and specified in an image." (See, Acts 14:8-20).

In God, there's the power to make us bear testimony of Him or not. That being that is not visible but becomes visible in the wisdom of how the creation is organized, "including us".

FAMILY CHAIN; MARIA, FELIX

Maria:

The chains represent generations that have lived in ignrance of God, inheriting a life of survival from our parents for generations. If one of these generations finds the understanding of the spirit that comes from the one and only God, this person begins the process of awakening to holiness. In addition, this person becomes the liberator of his descendants in the corporal, moral, and spiritual; with this, it is to say, (has broken the chain!)

In some cases, it occurs by the intervention of one of the family; for example, my father's families are Catholic, but unconsciously, I am referring to that they don't have an intense meditation on the existence of a God. Nevertheless, they seek to lead a proper life. While in my mother's family, my grandparents always spoke to us tirelessly about the wonders that God has always given us in the universe's creation and, as well as the conception of death, was because God allowed them. And that every human being has a sense of existence either at birth, during their life, or at death.

At that time, I was very young, time passed, and it seemed that all my uncles were leading an ordinary life even though it was the correct one. I was frustrated trying to understand the meaning of 'wait,' and I started to disregard their words. On the other hand, my grandmother spoke of the grace that brings patience, a concept I had no understanding of at the time. I tried to obtain it by being patient, but that helped me realize that it was not in me.

The true doctrine that was left implanted in my mind and heart was my grandmother's example of life. "She is a remarkably courageous woman in all aspects of lifework, love, patience, discipline, spirituality, and, above all, in helping others.

In the beginning, I thought that it was only education from their parents or theirs, like pride or dignity. Over time, I realized that her character was impressively stable. Without any kind of problem in good or bad times, my grandparents wouldn't change. To them, the grace before God is paramount, and they prioritize avoiding actions that would offend Him.

They both had a bit of difficult childhood at the beginning because they grew up in the Mexican Revolution. My grandmother was raised by her parents and siblings, but she never had the opportunity to meet her own grandparents. She is the youngest of all her family, and now she is the only one who lives, while my grandfather grew up with his mother and sister which were left orphans of a father. He didn't get to know the rest of his family because they were all scattered by the cause of the revolution, and nevertheless, they know how to read, write, mathematics, have all the sacraments, and possess many properties. For this reason, they serve as a living example that God comes first; they obey His commandments, remain faithful, and receive His sacraments.

They seemed humble and straightforward, but they possess a tireless spirit, responsible, full of grace, talented and wise, and by me still being young, I couldn't understand it. I even got to think that it was nothing more than just a suggestion or human habits. Now I know that is not so and that their being is not coincidental because they have a sense of existence in God.

When I learned God's purpose for all human beings, I also became aware of my sense of existence. I managed to position myself within the generational chain on my father's side and broke free from what bound me to them—the 'unconsciousness' that would have perpetuated their cycle with my own offspring.

I paid a heavy price, endured torment, and even faced death. In the end, I achieved freedom from that chain, bringing honor and happiness to my mother and her devout parents. For the loyalty of those who love God cannot be in vain. God is an all powerful, kind, and eternal deity for all of us. Now, I have a complete understanding of the great importance and value of the sacraments instituted in the Holy Church, both in their physical and spiritual aspects.

Felix:

I, Felix A. Gomez, have also broken the chain of one of my offspring. When I was seven or eight years old, I became aware that I lived in the countryside in my paternal grandparents' house in a small town called Down Hill Pananao in San José De Las Matas, Dominican Republic.

My grandparents have already passed over sixty years of age, Teofido and Luz Edubina Gomez. At that time, their children were already independent and married. I kept them company and helped them with the chores on the farm with agriculture and the farm's animals.

"The most that I remember from my grandparents is the faith and patience that they had in God. Every night around eight in the evening, I remember that we would start to prepare ourselves to go to sleep. The kitchen was separated to about one hundred feet away from the hut where we slept. The darkness was intense, especially on moonless nights. Without electricity in our town, we relied on gas lamps for light. When we came out of the kitchen, one could not even see their hands in front of them.

Before going to sleep every night, my grandparents and I dedicated ourselves to praying for a rosary. After haven finished the Rosary, we continued to thank God for all the requests that they had asked Him, and that God had granted them. Their faith in God was so great that they already considered it done when they asked for any requests.

I asked them how they knew when God had complied with their requests. My grandmother commented to me that we only had to have patience and wait, and when it arrived, we were going to notice it. My grandparents used to say, 'we know it is coming from God because He grants the requests of those who ask for good things, both for themselves and for others.'

For my upbringing and education in God, I will always be grateful to them for raising me in the Catholic faith and guiding me.

A confrontation that I experienced with one of my relatives led me to test the faith and patience that my grandparents had instructed me.

After this confrontation by the contrasts that I had with my relative, I coincided with meeting unexpectedly and witnessing the process of Maria's body and spiritual change, which experience led me to know of the existence of the chain. Thus, I got to know the chain of my offspring. And the experience from the process of forming the book led me to understand that the answers existed in the Holy Bible. I looked for the answers, and I meditated on them;

I came to comprehension and found my sense of existence. I liberated myself and gave thanks to God because this experience led me to understand God's will for me.

Furthermore, I also discovered that some negative attitudes inherited from my parents unconsciously were present in me, and I would then inherit them to my children to continue the chain. I continue locating these attitudes in able for me to eliminate them. I'm now looking for new positive habits.

"I've broken the generational chain that could have led me to commit misfortunes and devote myself to evil. Now I want to share my faith in God and my testimony!

WITCHCRAFT

Witches; supposedly endowed with certain magical abilities that are used with the intention of causing harm.

Witchcraft: The belief in the devil; formed by occult sects and pagan religions.

A pact with the devil; witches, fortunetellers, or sorcerers don't have any power beyond suggestion and instilling moral damage to the people they serve. Witches and sorcerers are people ensnared by suggestion, enslaved by immorality, and tasked with disseminating it. This way, so-called witches exploit their clients' frustrations for their advantage or benefit; this is known as fraud.

Sorcerers and fortunetellers harm themselves as well; since they devote their lives to this service, they forsake a healthy life and deprive themselves of a life of their own. They allow themselves to be used as puppets by something they truly don't know or understand. Its origin lies in the associations of witchcraft with devil worship, resulting in idolatry; (adoration to false gods).

The first step in the process of witchcraft is the association with the devil; the alleged witch has completed the process, pact, or agreement to learn her craft. "There is no good or white witchcraft; it is what it is, period."

Witchcraft involves a pact with the devil; during the pact, the witch agrees to worship the devil in exchange for acquiring supernatural powers, apparently, including the ability to cast various spells that can affect people.

Demonology: It comprises knowledge acquired by those who supposedly can invoke such entities, including instructions on how to summon demons, supposedly to subject them to the will of the conjurer. (The devil cannot be subjected to any person).

Modern witchcraft: This revolves around the figure of Satan or the devil, considered the god of pagans and witches. Witches held nocturnal meetings during which they worshiped the devil, and these gatherings were given various names, often involving rituals, crimes, and animal sacrifices. In reality, these practices were intended to desensitize the conscience and reduce mental meditation capacity.

In ancient times, the ritual symbolizing this satanic worship often involved abominable sexual acts and the use of drugs. These drugs included poisons from animals such as snakes and toads, as well as plants like mushrooms, which induced hallucinations, among others, disturbing all the senses.

Witchcraft proved attractive due to the prominent role it granted to women and their sexuality, leading to resistance against the Church and its teachings.

DEMONOLOGY

Demonology: It involves the belief in the existence of an evil entity that acts in opposition to the will of a God. The New Testament affirms the existence of minor spirits that are revealed and contrary to morality. The Old Testament presents Satan as a rebelled angel who is nevertheless submitted to the authority of God. Satan acts as a tempter, seeking to cast doubt on virtue and provoke all kinds of evils. It also mentions the existence of hell inhabited by demons who accuse and torment the sinners who fall there, as well as tempt mortals or act to disturb them.

Satan: Known as the adversary, the enemy, the accuser, or the slanderer. In the New Testament, the origin of Satan is explained; he was one of God's angels who turned evil. This means that he was once a spiritual creature who belonged to God's angelic family. His name was changed to Satan because he went against God's will, desiring the adoration that all intelligent creatures were giving to the Creator. He was the angel who guarded God's throne, often referred to as God's first son, Lucifer. However, due to his pride and ambition to become another god, he was cast out of heaven along with other angels who later rebelled (demons). (See Genesis 6:1-2, Revelation 12:7-9, and 12:3-4).

The origin of the devil, Satan, the former bearer of light, at some point becomes contrary, transitioning into darkness, and forever ceases to be part of the light.

The victory of God over the devil was ultimately achieved through the crucifixion of Jesus. Jesus confirmed the existence of evil and marked two eras: a thousand years of light and a thousand years of darkness. * Evil starts to strengthen at the beginning of its time and reaches its peak at the end of the two eras*.

The Gospel: It conveys a dual message to humanity, serving as both a warning to be vigilant against the snares of evil and a set of teachings. The Gospel's texts often present narrations or statements that are indirectly directed towards Satan, though they are understood by humans. (See Isaiah 14:12-15). These messages carry a double meaning, addressing Satan while being applicable to humans. To comprehend these texts fully, it is essential to consider our human and spiritual state.

A faithful person has God within them, radiating more light and purity, and they are led by the Spirit of God, the Holy Spirit. (See Romans 7:1-25 and 8:1-27). This Spirit of God takes control of the body by acknowledging its weaknesses and temptations, guiding individuals in the grace to avoid things that may lead them astray and jeopardize their place in heaven.

"Who exercises justice is fair and is of God." (Galatians 3: 26-29).

The devil continually seeks to influence people's consciousness: **"Be alert, because our adversary, the devil, walks about seeking whom he may devour."** (See Genesis 4: 6-7 and 1Peter 5:1-11).

"Lest be that led by our pride, come to fall into the same condemnation in which the devil fell", Satan primarily acts on the consciences of those in positions of power.

He also preys on those who lack knowledge of God. **"There is among them a spirit of corruption; they do not know the Lord"** (Hosea 5: 4-11).

"Since his fall, the devil has continued to sin through humans who allow themselves to be influenced by him."

"Whoever commits sin, from the devil is." (1John 3: 7-10) This does not necessarily mean they are condemned to evil or hell but that the person is in a critical state.

When the devil becomes the guide of a person, they will carry out his will, becoming a unit (John 6:70-71, and for further reflection, see 1 Corinthians 12:12-31).

The antichrists form one body/group, a beast, since by not believing in their spiritual state, they live a life dominated by their physical body. The devil exploits this ignorance and our weaknesses so that he may live.

Some of the most common names for the devil include "Devil, Lucifer, Satan, the seducer, the devourer, grand dragon, the dark God, or father of the Lie." Satan signifies an obstacle or pursuer.

Satan spiritually accuses humanity of evil inclinations and actions before God. He also accuses individuals on the day of their death (individual's spiritual judgment) in an attempt to secure their condemnation and subject them to torment.

Satan sought authorization to test Job's faith. (See Job 1:1-22 and 2:1-10). In this story, the righteous man is afflicted, revealing that divine justice is inscrutable.

Satan is responsible for the evil inclinations within all humans, causing afflictions and misfortunes. Thus, individuals may conclude that there is no existence of a God. By distancing ourselves willfully from God, Satan takes possession of us through our ignorance. His objective is to gain dominion over this world, focusing on the living, both in spirit and body, rather than those who are already dead.

ANTICHRIST

Antichrist: It references to the manifestation predicted for the end of time and the anticipation of this manifestation in the action of people who disavow Christianity. "The Antichrist," those who are against Christianity, could be anyone opposed to the Messiah and what He represents.

Dear children, this is the last hour; and as you have heard that the antichrist is coming, even now many antichrists have come. This is how we know it is the last hour. (1John 2:18-29, 3:1-24 and 4:1-21).

"Whoever is not with me is against me...."Luke 11:23

"The Antichrist will appear as a man controlled by Satan. He will be evil incarnate, the man of sin, the son of perdition."

This will be due to several factors, including the rise of occultism, declines in morality and values, during a period called "the great tribulation" (the test for all, the time to decide whether one will do good or evil).

In the words of Jesus in the Gospels, many will also claim to be the Messiah and Savior. Anyone can be an Antichrist, provided that, despite being a confessed Christian, they go against Christ.

"They claim to be inspired by the Devil and possess the ability to oppose God, commit evil, and assert that there is no God to judge them."

(The Antichrist: Those who form a united opposition against God; this opposition exists because these people do not believe in their spiritual condition).

It is also concluded that anyone, whether familiar with the Gospel or not, who refuses to acknowledge that Jesus is the Christ, denies His divinity or His resurrection, and believes that there is only one form of human reality (the physical), embodies the spirit of Antichrist, particularly when it comes to contempt for Christian doctrine.

The devil always hides and takes on forms that appear innocuous, as exemplified next by "Vampirism."

VAMPIRES

Personify mainly to unconscious forms representing the repressed and hidden human instincts or impulses, often more primitive, tracing back to the beginning. They are seen as incarnations of evil entities, symbolizing the wild, beastly side of humanity (all physical aspects). Vampires are a complex combination of various human fears and beliefs, often rooted in the fear of untamed instincts.

Attribution to blood: The belief that blood is an instrument of power, with the idea that by consuming it, one can obtain the skills or powers of the victim.

Fear of predation: Fear of diseases or death, with a tangible expression, often resembling that of a corpse.

Vampire: The term is used to describe someone akin to a corpse, believed to be devoid of a soul, destined for darkness, drawn to impurity, and possessing a passion for blood.

In conclusion, the existence of demons on Earth remains unverified. Rather, it is the human spirit's attempt to convey its state of darkness through the unconscious mind. If the conscious mind fails to recognize and address this darkness in time, individuals may lose control over their actions, leading to a loss of mental balance. Such impulsive acts could jeopardize their lives and their place in the kingdom of God, both in ancient times and in the present day.

Vampires were often likened to witches or individuals who had rebelled against the Church because, while they were still alive, they had embraced paganism. This was seen as a way of giving their souls to the devil, allowing demons to possess their bodies and use them as instruments to cause disturbances and spread evil in the world, often teaching immoral practices and promoting malevolence.

Regarding life after death, it was believed that after the body's corruption and having obtained the survival of the soul until Judgment Day, there was a possibility of accessing the light. This was thought to be the fate of those who had died repentant of their sins and had received the Sacraments.

Vampires: the existence of demons that change form; demons vampires, a tormented spirit with a hunger for repugnant substances or blood, which makes it dangerous for the living, the innocents.

Vampires were seen as entities connected to the cult of the ancestors, which was part of the persistent paganism of some cultures, causing concern for others. The demon within the vampire was described as thirsty for innocent blood, driven by the demon of vanity, leading to unimaginable acts and growing stronger with each passing day. This involved a disregard for God's will and the talents and gifts provided by God for us to live and glorify Him.

Humanity often categorizes what they don't understand as mental disorders, which serves as an easier explanation for them. They assigned vampirism a specific category, distinguishing it from other conditions such as necrophilia (a morbid attraction to death or some of its aspects) or sadism. This was done to better describe the criminal conduct motivated by <u>libidinous pleasure</u> (adjective) "lustfully inclined, weak to sexual pleasures", derived from seeing, contacting, or drinking the blood of their victims.

"All these issues can be controlled through prayer, a healthy and nutritious diet, and by mentally rejecting false ideas, no matter how fascinating they might seem. Paganism is one sufficient cause to weaken these and other similar groups. Two ways of excluding yourself from God are, either through the desires of the heart or feelings of unworthiness before God".

GANGS

Many impoverished and orphaned children survived by joining gangs that are controled by criminal adults. These gangs are notorious for engaging in various criminal activities, primarily drug trafficking, and a significant portion of their income is derived from the illegal drug trade.

In many cases, prison gangs require their members to get tattoos, and some groups even demand that prospective members shed blood from another person as a prerequisite for joining. Such initiation rituals often involve the requirement of an assassination as a pact of blood or as proof of loyalty. Modern gangs have also introduced new acts of violence, which could be used as an initiation ceremony for the new members. This can be likened to elements of satanic idolatry, where members are bound by an unwavering commitment to the gang, with the penalty for renouncing being death.

Members of these gangs are typically young. Many of them have struggled in school, with a considerable number abandoning their education altogether. Often, they have relatives who were or are involved in gangs as well. These young individuals frequently lack consistent adult supervision from an early age. They seek acceptance, companionship, protection, recognition, and a sense of belonging, which they find in gangs. Their shared experiences of neglect and deprivation lead them to form these groups. Gangs often exert maximum control over urban, impoverished communities, where many of these youths may not have been exposed to alternatives or to God's teachings.; (these are youngsters that don't know how to reject evil because they don't know God).

Other gangs originated in prisons or from the Department of Juvenile Corrections, and right from inside the jail, most of them continue running their gangs.

All these issues and more stem from a rejection of God and an involuntary covenant with the devil through impurity. It is exacerbated by ignorance of God's existence, passed down through generations.

Gangs represent another form of idolatry, entwining lives and those of their children with impurity, fueled by inadequate nourishment, alcohol, drugs, and behaviors that erode consciousness and selfworth. This cycle leads to suffering, resentment, and a loss of faith in God, as well as hope for a dignified life in harmony. In God, there is purpose and a solution to all these problems, but without knowledge of God, life may appear meaningless, and value may not be attached to it. This is a reminder that we have only one life in this physical body, and our time is finite. It serves as a warning that when we eventually come to our senses, it may be too late to make amends.

ALL SAINTS' DAY

All Saints' Day: is a Catholic tradition instituted in honor of all the Saints, both known and unknown. Considering that each martyr should be recognized, the Church has designated one day for this purpose.

Saints, whom we have had the opportunity to know, have been depicted in images for recognition and to remember their holiness through their examples and works. These individuals serve as examples that one can achieve a state of holiness. This holiness is more widely recognized in the Catholic Church because it is understood that the person has attained communion with God and strives to understand life itself.

"The saints" throughout their entire lives pointed out how they found the way to God in certain situations. They invite us to pray so that we too can draw closer to God. Holiness is accessible to everyone; it is the perfection to which we are all entitled. Holiness is a spiritual journey, and the reward is received in heaven.

Holiness must be proclaimed so that it can touch the hearts of those who yearn for it, especially for the thirsty spirits of God's love. True love comes solely from God; it is a love that does not covet sharing the glory of God (See John 3:14-21).

THE IMAGE OF DEATH

It is rather due to the prayers from the rite of the sacrament of the anointing of the sick, in which one asks God for a Holy death. This means to die in friendship with God, in case the patient is in a terminal condition. A holy death, in religious interpretation, involves Catholics performing a prayer to receive a holy death in a state of total resignation. This death is as worthy as that of a saint (specifically reserved for the faithful or those converted to the one and only God). It's another form of prayer in case one might be in a situation where they could lose their life. (The prayer is to always devote the soul to God).

The Catholic Church has rejected devotion to shadowy statues. In pagan culture, they have created a figure to which they give offerings: a skeleton covered with a tunic, concealing everything except the face and hands. This figure invites worshippers to rituals that lead to delinquency. It's one more image of idolatry, another guise of the devil. It originates from the disturbance caused by sin, ignorance, and impurity. On having asked for favors, they essentially become sons of the death, allowing the devil to manipulate them for his work, infusing them with hatred, envy, sadness, inferiority, and other negative emotions. This image of death is simply a more subtle way of disguising the sense of hell and satanic services. In this way, conceals; it doesn't evoke as much fear.

Similar to the practices of Santeria, they sacrifice and offer gifts to the rulers of the abyss. Over time, these offering practices continue to persist, "and nowadays, with the image of the holy death." By their own volition, they surrender their lives, bodies, and souls to the darkness, in the service of the demon, accepting death as their father (the Ancient Serpent). (See Mark 13:14).

The demons to whom the idolatrous people serve delight in the bad intentions and impurity of the blood offered in sacrifices. And if these people don't offer sacrifices, these demons take their sacrifices through perturbation, causing misfortunes such as hatred, jealousy, envy, suicide, and taking their souls in impurity, thus gaining them in darkness for the realm of Darkness.

Through idolatry, the rebellious Angels expand their territory, gaining power over sinners and taking possession of their souls. Idolatry invites impurity, which is the first act that God forbids.

There is someone more powerful than death: "The Christ!" Jesus overcame the temptation of the body, which means controlling disordered desires that lead to impurity and cause indignation, distancing us from God.

Through Eve, death gained power in humanity until the end of its generation. Thus, everyone will face temptation, and this is where the ordeal lies—to make us holy or conscious. Anyone who proves victorious will enter the Kingdom of light and have the right to be a son of God in spiritual purity (God is light!) (See Revelation 2:7, 2:17, 3:5, 3:21, and 3:12).

Death: "Also known as the Ancient Serpent, the Prince of Darkness, the son of Lucifer — the father of all who live in darkness, lovers of darkness and everything it contains."

AGAINST NATURAL

Homosexuality is defined as interaction, "the union btween individuals of the same sex, regardless of gender." In international scientific terms, it is considered that homosexuality is not a disease or a disorder that needs to be cured. The homosexual condition should be first understood as mental, as the existence of homosexual practice deviates from natural and normal behavior due to experiences during development in infancy, influences, and drugs.

Homosexuality is a disturbance that should also be considered with the importance it deserves and be treated, corrected, or cared for in private counseling coupled with its fundamental development. (Homosexuality: lack of psychological and sexual development, related to the mind). The fear of not feeling sufficiently sexually instructed can provoke insecurity that could lead to homosexuality, as individuals experiment with mutual pleasure in an attempt to mature sexually. It is not a habit of degeneration or disease; rather, it is an idea of insecurity that leads to a certain lifestyle.

At present, many people are no longer pretending or repressing their sexual orientation, and there are many who openly embrace their sexual orientation. It is not due to social repression that denies homosexuality, but to what homosexuality itself represents to transgender individuals, a condition of incompatibility (it's not one or the other).

Homosexuality: an expression of degeneration (thoughts of immorality), often involuntary and originating from situations unrelated to the individual, such as drugs, rape, influences from others, etc. For example, it can result in perversions, sexual aberrations, or sadistic or masochistic practices. It refers to unnatural sexual acts committed between women, between persons of the male sex, or between humans and animals. (See Romans 1:21-32).

Regarding the roles taken by transgender individuals, one man may take on the role of the male, while the other assumes the role of the woman. This also applies to lesbians; one may simulate characteristics such as muscles, attitude, and wear more masculine clothing, and is considered "active" or "manly," while the other may present as more feminine and is considered "passive." In reality, no transgender person is exclusively active or passive throughout their lifetime; their role may change over time.

HOMOPHOBIA

Homophobia is often used to describe those who oppose certain civil laws, particularly those related to people of different sexual orientations. It has, at times, been misapplied to label anyone who objects to inappropriate behaviors or certain attitudes of transgender individuals for moral reasons. It's essential to recognize that this objection isn't homophobia but rather an equally respectable opinion based on different principles. Therefore, it should not be categorized as homophobia. (Transgender individuals have made choices regarding their homosexuality or lack thereof, *exercising their Free Will*, a capacity that has existed since the beginning of humanity). See Ecclesiasticus 15:11-20.

SODOMY

Sodomite: Historically, this term was used to describe men who engaged in sexual relationships with other men, often with the connotation of being submissive to the dominant partner. Some also applied this term to women who practiced anal intercourse, associating it with being 'sullied,' 'submissive,' and losing control over themselves.

In ancient times, sodomy was linked to witchcraft derived from idolatry, particularly in the context of demon worship. sodomy leads to cases of violations, with the main risk to children.

Lesbians who possess the sin of pride and who want to dominate others, including challenging or trying to equalize the male, would also vary their role); so, this would also fall under sodomy. (Both fall into prostitution by the lack of control from their passions).

Many people believe they can control their attitudes and behaviors by setting personal limits. However, these passions can sometimes feel like an endless abyss, where one inclination leads to another. As the saying goes, 'He who believes he can dominate evil deceives himself.'

PROSTITUTION

Prostitution is defined as the act of participating in sexual activities in exchange for money or goods, even though individuals of both sexes engage in this activity. Prostitution can involve both heterosexual and homosexual interactions. Men, women, and lesbians, who primarily offer their services to men, also engage in threesomes and orgies. Prostitution is the act of dedicating oneself to having intercourse with others in exchange for money and is considered, in essence, like any other form of remuneration.

In prostitution, there is no existence of any emotional connection or relationship in the person who engages in it. This definition also encompasses the use of sex as a means of espionage, gaining fame, or seeking recognition. For instance, this can be observed in cases where individuals maintain relationships with famous people with the intention of selling their stories to the press in exchange for money or fame.

Prostitution and crime: Within the realm of prostitution, there are also instances of drug distribution, assaults on clients, extortion, demands for luxury items, and other associated crimes.

Prostitution since ancient times: Prostitution has earned the distinction of being considered the world's oldest profession. It has been known practically since the advent of historical records and has been practiced in all societies. Ancient historians have documented the existence of prostitution in Babylon, where women would enter the sanctuary to engage in sexual acts with foreigners as a sign of hospitality in exchange for symbolic payment (See Revelation 14: 8). Prostitution was practiced by both women and young men and was also carried out as a religious rite in honor of idols.

In Israel, prostitution was common even though it was expressly forbidden by Jewish law. Prophets like Jeremiah (Jeremiah 2: 20-25, 5: 7-9 and 13:10) was opposed to it (See, 1Kings 15: 9-13, Leviticus 20: 13); will encounter the first death, the spiritual, which is to live among evil and for evil. (Revelation 20: 6).

(This has its primary origin in idolatry or paganism; it is equivalent to distancing us from God and not knowing His words to learn what He has for us. The perturbation blinds us not to see that there is more than just flesh and that within each of us lives a spirit that comes from God.

Asa did what God regards as right, as his ancestor David had done. He drove the male prostitutes out of the country and got rid of all the idols which his

ancestors had made. He even deprived his grandmother Maacah of the dignity of Great Lady for having made an obscenity for Asherah; Asa cut down her obscenity and burnt it in the ravine of the Kidron.
(1Kings 15: 11-13)

Kidnapping: Where do the children (boys and girls) exploited in prostitution come from? The number of allegations of disappearances of minors has multiplied. Cases of child prostitution are terrible and, unfortunately, are real, occurring over the past years. Child prostitution conceals much more; these children and youngsters are enslaved and forced to be objects for sexual use. This kind of prostitution is not voluntary. It is accompanied by the fear of hunger, dependency on drugs, and a host of circumstances that can turn the existence of a minor and an adult into absolute hell. These networks of minors' corruption are discovered and dismantled by the authorities, from which they also seize thousands of photographs and pornographic videos of children. Minors who escape from their houses could also end up in one of these organizations. (See, Matthew 18:2-10). **Because, The Son of Man has come to save what has been lost (11).**

The prostitutes and male prostitutes usually maintain relations with many customers. Prostitution is associated with the spread of

Sexually Transmitted Diseases; among these, AIDS currently poses a greater risk of contagion. (First, they fall into spiritual illness; they don't realize that the spirit given to us by God lives in us) (Genesis 2:20-24 and 1Corinthians 6:12-20).

Currently, from what we could personally observe, it looks like new forms of prostitution have been imposed. One of them is the famous delivery (home delivery service), where organizations in prostitution make distributions of girls or a girl for service in the home of a client or clients. Sometimes, a single girl prostitutes herself with the people in an apartment or house. The number of people typically varies between five or more individuals; it's "a wellorganized service for obtaining customers."

We also observed another form of prostitution. A woman who has a regular daily job also has several clients to whom she offers her home delivery services for money or goods like clothes, jewelry, food, help with rent payments, etc.

Felix comments: "During my tenure as a manager at a company, I encountered several women who had five to six children from different men. They would take legal action against each of the children's fathers, compelling them to provide monthly maintenance for their respective offspring and, as well as seeking government assistance. The support amount for a single child was calculated to be around one fourth of the father's weekly wage or more. Regrettably, it seemed that their primary concern was their own benefit, with little regard for the future that awaited the children."

MARY MAGDALENA

According to the Gospel of Luke, Mary Magdalene hosted and provided material support to Jesus and his disciples during his preaching in Galilee, along with her siblings Lazarus and Martha. It is also mentioned that Jesus had previously cured her. She fell into temptations from the demons who sought to ruin her Holy family. After her release from the demons, she also accompanied Jesus and the twelve apostles, as well as several other women who had been healed from evil spirits and diseases. Mary, named Magdalene, from whom seven demons had been cast out.

Christianity holds Mary Magdalene in particular esteem for her closeness to Jesus, considering her equal to the Apostles. Before meeting Jesus, she had lived a life of sin (libertine). The Catholic Church does not assert that she had been involved in prostitution. This idea originates from the identification of Mary with the sinner in passages like Luke 7:36-50 and 8:2, where it is said, this time clearly referring to Mary Magdalene, that seven demons had been cast out from her. Nothing in these passages leads to the conclusion that Mary Magdalene was dedicated to prostitution; *she was a lost sheep.*

After Jesus' ascension, Mary Magdalene repented and spent the rest of her life in a cave, engaging in prayers, penance, and severe fasting to mortify her flesh. She is identified here as Mary of Bethany, where she is believed to have lived a life of penance for 30 years. When the time of her death arrived, her spirit was carried away by angels, and her body was buried in a chapel built by Maximo in Villa Lata.

Jesus has defended us through the personality of Mary Magdalene. Jesus doesn't distinguish between men and women. He sees the beauty of purity in the spirit and the intentions stored in the heart. He has infinite love for each of us and desires us to be with Him in the house of God, our Father. However, there is no place for corruption in heaven. God is so compassionate that He continually and promptly provides us with the solution to rid ourselves, if we desire, of what is displeasing to Him so that we can share His Kingdom. He is a God that rejects evil because it is irritating by the unbearable pestilence of its corruption. In God, there's the power to make us bear testimony of Him and as well as the testimony of other Saints through their great repentance, penance, and amendment for their sins, as God did with "Salomon".

KING SALOMON

The attribute of Solomon is of righteousness and justice."
Solomon: Described in the Bible for his wisdom, wealth, and power, was the wisest man who existed on Earth. He built the Temple of Jerusalem and is credited with authoring books found in the Bible. He is the protagonist of many legends.

Solomon was the second of the sons that King David and Bathsheba had. In the Bible, the Prophet Nathan informed David that God had commanded the death of his first son as punishment for the King's sin. David had sent Uriah to his death, who was Bathsheba's husband, so that the King could marry her (2 Samuel 12:14). This was because David had despised the precepts of God. After a week of prayer and fasting, David heard the news of his son's death and comforted Bathsheba, who immediately became pregnant, this time with Solomon. Solomon then replaced and succeeded his father, David.

In the Bible, it is written that God appeared to Solomon and said to him: **"Ask for what you want me to give you."**

Solomon said: "Gives to your servant a docile heart to judge your people, to discern between good and evil".

God answered: "I have done according to your Words, behold, I have given you wise and understanding heart". (Such wisdom was based on following the commandments of God). Solomon loved God, walking in the counseling of his father, David.

Solomon consolidated Israel's dominion in the region and surrounded himself with all kinds of luxuries. However, in the middle of his reign, he gave in to idolatry, induced by his numerous foreign wives. Solomon built temples for other gods. He inherited a large empire conquered by his father, King David. He possessed a harem of women, including the daughter of the Pharaoh (1 Kings 3:1, 1:1-12, and 9:16-18). Both the king and his people were devoted to trade and were ensnared by the ambition of wealth, falling into materialism (Nehemiah 13:26, Psalms 53:3-4, and Jeremiah 5:24-27).

Although he sinned, falling into vanity caused by impurity and perturbation, he later repented and wrote the books of Proverbs and Wisdom to advise against following his example of clumsiness, (all this come from the traps of the demons). Solomon wrote these books as a testimony and as an example that things of this world are momentary.

"God's commandments make the ingenious one, Wise".

DEATH

Death: The judgment in which the conscience is open, and the spirit is judged according to the book of life, *The Bible*. Jesus, the witness of the flesh and the spirit, evaluates our works individually, and He is the righteous judge.

At the moment of the agony of death, we relive our life from old age back to childhood and birth. When entering the dimension of death, we retrospectively revisit life, but in a rapid and intense manner. All the atoms of information are contained in both bodies, with clear and precise memories of childhood, adolescence, youth, maturity, old age, and decrepitude. The individual sees their entire life in the form of images, in a retrospective order. These memories are also found in the spiritual body, and the being relives each scene of life, experiencing joy for the good deeds and deep moral pain for the bad ones. After finishing this retrospective journey, we gain complete awareness of the results of the life that has just passed.

Each atom of the spiritual body penetrates within every atom of the physical body; this is how we turn out to be alive. The spiritual body has more reality than the physical body. The physical body totally changes during the course of life; the spiritual body does not change.

In reality, the spirit is the most important aspect of the physical body. At the last moment of life, the soul, or spirit departs from the physical body with profound agony during the dying process. The spiritual body does not enter the grave. The spiritual body is consent to the reality of the place appointed by the life it had led, leaving the physical body in total unconsciousness without sense. Without the spirit, the physical body undergoes an inevitable state of decomposition. "Spirit"; vital energy for the body, which is always conscious. (For further reflection, see 1Corintians 15:1-58).

THE JUDGMENT

The judgment: Our conscience and internal judgment begin. When someone dies, they enter another dimension. Eternity opens to receive the agonizing soul, concluding the retrospective examination. In this new dimension, we must appear in a celestial court, where saints and demons are present. We are summoned to answer the charges presented by the demons, who aim to claim the soul of the defendant for eternal torment. Ultimately, we face the judgment of the righteous judge, Jesus Christ.

Hell, Earth, or Heaven: The judgment distinguishes between those who will immediately reincarnate and those who will not. The agonizing souls are cast out, destined to return to the world of time and matter. They are returned only to their own bodies, removed from eternity because they have not yet become a definitively "good or bad being." Only those who possess a clearly defined "being," whether good or bad, can reside in eternity. The judgment separates those who reincarnate immediately because they have not yet earned their place in their eternal destination. "The being" refers to the nature of their spirit as either good or bad. When they find themselves at the threshold of life and death, this judgment determines their fate. If their place is found in eternity, the person will die.

Those condemned to hell will endure unbearable suffering, and it is eternal, free from the constraints of time. During their earthly lives, these individuals no longer respond to any form of correction or punishment. They are dedicated to perpetrating evil deeds and derive pleasure from wickedness, becoming passionate about sinful desires. Their persistent criminal behavior is a consequence of their excessive materialism.

Those who ascend to paradise experience a state that defies description. To the extent that I have perceived it, I can only convey that it is a state of supreme joy and peace.

"The law of action and consequence" dictates that to change our external circumstances, we must first undergo internal transformation. We must transmute and refine our base qualities, turning them from vices into virtues, from impurities into holiness, as if we were turning base metals into gold and diamonds. As our consciousness awakens, we become aware of the mysteries of life and death."

BOOK OF THE DEAD

Book of the dead: "To rise to the day," is an expression of the concept of death as understood in the most ancient times we have records of, particularly in Ancient Egypt.

Regeneration, Triumph, and Joy: This signifies the importance of triumphing over internal enemies, such as false feelings and spiritual demons. "To rise to the day" also conveys a sense of transfiguration, representing a way to express what awaits in the day of death with complete resignation and inner peace.

"To be able to manifest itself in diverse forms, to use the solar barge, and to acquire knowledge of certain mysteries before entering the tomb" is an expression from ancient Egypt that underscores the power and advantage of being alive. It emphasizes the need to raise awareness during life to attain ultimate dignity, even in death.

Judgment before the Definitive Tribunal of the Holy Almighty: In this phase, the agonizer or deceased stands before the tribunal where their heart, conscience, morality, intentions, and their deeds are weighed. This is the moment when the negative confessions and declarations of innocence, presented by the agonizer or deceased, are examined in an attempt to justify their actions. If they pass this test, they can continue their journey towards the light, avoiding eternal disapproval.

The significance of this judgment lies in the fact that the heart is weighed against the good and bad deeds, a detail rooted in ancient history. It serves as a testament to the belief in an afterlife, emphasizing that one cannot live a life in vain. As human beings, our morality in life carries consequences beyond the earthly realm.

JESUS OF NAZARETH

The pregnancy of Mary was the result of the work of the Holy Spirit, as prophesied in the words of the Prophet Isaiah (Isaiah 7:14), which stated that "her child would be the Messiah awaited by the Jews" (Matthew 1:19-21).

The emperor ordered the first census, requiring everyone to register in their place of birth. As Joseph was a native of Bethlehem, they had to travel there. Jesus was born in Bethlehem during their journey. This occurrence highlights how God orchestrates every situation to fulfill the prophecies of the Holy Scriptures through His prophets (Luke 2:1-7).

Wise kings from the East, guided by both prophecies and the alignment of planets (Stars), arrived in Jerusalem seeking the newborn King of the Jews to worship Him. Their inquiry alerted King Herod of Judea, who was used as an instrument by evil due to his wicked heart. Herod decided to eliminate the potential rival, as mentioned in Revelation 12:3-4.

The Kings or monarchs, guided by the star, eventually arrived in Bethlehem and worshipped the child. This star, which shines every 2,000 years, serves as a sign of the Millennium belonging to God. It signifies the immense power of God, as the entire universe gives Him glory and honor. Jesus, also known as Christ, is the Son in whom God is well pleased due to His total obedience. He taught us through the prayer of "Our Father" and His teachings that He is the Son of God. A sign in the sky to reminds us that God is eternal and never abandons us, even though time passes for us, for God, doesn't.

Once again, an angel visited Joseph (Matthew 2:13-14) and warned him of Herod's inevitable persecution. The family fled to Egypt and remained there until the death of the monarch, as referenced in Revelation 12:6. Once again, God notified Joseph through the Angel, which appears before him for the third time; the waiting is highlighted in absolute faith, which would never be disappointed (Matthew 2:19-23).

The story of the conception of Jesus is intertwined with that of John the Baptist. Elizabeth, the mother of John the Baptist, and Mary, Jesus's mother, are relatives. Both Jesus and John had their conceptions announced by the angel Gabriel. John the Baptist was a prophesied messenger sent to herald the arrival of Jesus and to initiate the baptism symbolizing renewal and the beginning of the Church of Jesus (Luke 1:5-25, 1:39-80, Mark 1:2-4, and John 1:1-18).

The Annunciation (Luke 1:26-38) is a pivotal moment where God, through the Holy Spirit, promises the Virgin Mary the fulfillment of the prophecy, which is Jesus—this marks the first revelation of the Holy Trinity.

In the Gospels of Matthew and Luke, two genealogies of Jesus are presented (Matthew 1:1-16 and Luke 3:23-38). These genealogies trace Jesus's lineage through figures such as Patriarch Abraham, Adam, and David. However, it's important to note that these genealogies are associated with Joseph and Mary.

John the Baptist, Jesus's cousin, prophesied the evangelization of Jesus and baptized Him in the Jordan River. During this baptism, the Spirit of God descended upon Jesus in the form of a dove, and God's voice was heard, revealing the Holy Trinity.

Following His baptism, the Spirit led Jesus to the desert, where He fasted for forty days and overcame the temptations presented by the devil "propositions" to which the demon submitted him: (Ephesians 6:10-18). He was not the exception.

All four Gospels narrate that Jesus rose from the dead on the third day after His crucifixion. An earthquake occurred, and an angel dressed in white rolled away the stone from the Tomb. The guards, who witnessed this event, were overcome with fear and appeared as if they were dead (Matthew 28:1-14). The angel then announced to the women the resurrection of Jesus.

The authors of the New Testament narrate the life of Jesus, and their testimonies converge on one central figure: Jesus. He is the fulfillment of the prophecies found in the books of the Old Testament. The earlier Christians were chosen to bring these prophecies to fruition, as foretold in the writings of Isaiah, Jeremiah, Zechariah, Psalms, and Micah. The arrival of Jesus of Nazareth was the long-awaited Messiah anticipated by the people of Israel, and His life and death align with these prophecies.

Every aspect of His life, including the role of John the Baptist and the location of Jesus's birth, His passion, death, and sacrificial role as God's servant crucified during the era of Pontius Pilate, had been prophesied. These references provide undeniable evidence of the existence of Jesus.

In ancient times, the earliest Christian writings primarily expressed the faith of Christians in God, with secondary emphasis on providing biographical information about Jesus. This faith in Jesus Christ has been so profound that it has shaped our calendar, distinguishing between the years before Christ (B.C.) and those after Christ (A.D.).

The first day of the week in the Old Testament, now known as Sunday, held special significance, which was carried forward into the New Testament. In the Old Testament, it was the seventh day,

Saturday, that marked the day of rest as a sign between God and Israel. The order was clear: work for six days and then rest on the seventh, which is why it's known as Saturday, meaning 'rest.

Today, in the time of the Church, which corresponds to the Exemption of Grace, we place our confidence in the unique and perfect work accomplished by the Lord Jesus Christ on the cross at Calvary for our salvation. As Christians, we dedicate our lives to Him, seeking His glory, expressing gratitude from our fruitful hearts, and demonstrating our faith through good works. God has promised us heaven as a reward for our devotion. Let us trust in our Lord Jesus Christ for our salvation!

Sunday, the day of Jesus Christ's resurrection, holds special significance. It symbolizes endurance through afflictions and the fulfillment of His ministry. The Crown of Righteousness, promised by the righteous Judge, the Lord, awaits us.

Traditionally, Sunday is considered the seventh day of the week, with the week starting on Monday and ending on Sunday. Jesus reestablished the significance of the seventh day as a day of rest and honor to God, having triumphed over the works of evil, which are now symbolized on day six. Sunday is celebrated as a holiday or festively in most countries around the world and is part of the weekend. The name 'Sunday' originates from the Latin 'Lord's Day,' reflecting the Christian celebration of Jesus.

It is written that Jesus, as Son of Man, is the Lord of Saturday. Some early Christians observed Saturday, while others gathered to worship on Sunday; it is the day when God created light.

Christians worship God the first day of the week: **Remember the Sabbath day,** (Saturday) **to keep it Holy.** The day of rest was created for communion with God and humanity. (Exodus 20: 81-1)

"Jesus and Saturday: The law was given through Moses, but grace and truth have come to us through Jesus Christ. (John 1:10-17)

Jesus taught His disciples that He is the Lord of the Day of Rest. Both Jesus and His disciples worked on Saturday, the Day of Rest, and because of this, some considered that Jesus had desecrated Saturday. Jesus proclaimed Himself as God, and for these reasons, some sought to kill Him.

Jesus Christ particularly emphasized Sunday for His resurrection and for special gatherings with His disciples.

The following Scriptures explain why Christians gather on Sunday to worship God. Jesus was resurrected from the dead on the first day of the week, , after Saturday, at dawn (Matthew 28:1, Mark 16:2, Luke 24:1, and John 20:1).

The Church's inception occurred on the first day of the week. God directed Peter to preach to the Gentiles, who were new believers and not Jews. They did not practice circumcision, rest on a Saturday, or observe other Jewish traditions. Guided by the Holy Spirit, this decision contributed to unity within the Catholic Church.

As stated in Matthew 21:43, Jesus foretold; **I tell you, then, that the Kingdom of God will be taken from you and given to people who will produce its fruit.**

The great responsibility of those called to work in the Lord's vineyard varies with each epoch, but it primarily involves promoting and renewing complete fidelity to Christ. Despite Jesus Christ's rejection and crucifixion, His resurrection brings absolute confidence, and the foundation of every human existence can be anchored in Him. This truth is echoed in the parable of the vineyard workers, where the vineyard owner represents God (See Matthew 20:1-16).

Jesus also grants us the gift of life, empowering us to do good through His grace and our commitment. Regrettably, human impurity often leads to infidelity and a rejection of God. Pride and selfishness can blind us to the most precious gift from God, His only begotten Son in the faith—Christ. Remaining in Him, solely in Him, for Him, and by Him, is how the Church is built, forming the people of the new Covenant. The Lord is perpetually near and actively involved in the history of humanity."

"The reality belongs to Christ because the Kingdom of God is not about indulging in the pleasures of material things but rather about upholding justice, fostering peace, and embracing joy in the Holy Spirit. Those who serve Christ in this way are preserving God's presence and gaining approval from their neighbors. Therefore, let us pursue actions that contribute to peace and mutual edification (See 1 Corinthians 9:20-27).

It is written: by my own life says the Lord, every knee shall bow before me, every tongue shall give glory to God. It is to God, then, that each of us will have to give an account of himself. Romans 14: 11-12 "It is our duty to receive the weak in faith with understanding."

The Gospel portrays Jesus as a preexistent being substantially united with God, sent by Him to save humanity from 'Original Sin,' atoning for it with His blood, bearing witness to the one and only God, and restoring His people. In this mission, He established His Church, providing everything necessary for our salvation.

"In the realm of Christian Catholic theology, Jesus the Christ embodies a profound unity. He is Jesus as a human being and Christ as the divine idea, representing God's purpose with humanity.

Christ spirit: With the ascension, physical Jesus was perpetuated in the human essence and with the spiritual identity continued existing in the eternal order in the form of divine science, redeeming the world's sins.

It is essential to clarify that Jesus is not God but the Son of God, sharing a unity in quality with God, not quantity. God primarily serves as a spiritual savior, with a secondary corporal aspect. Salvation is not merely achieved through forgiveness but involves a transformative process and a spiritual resource, driven by the need for peace through faith in God.

Hymns are sung to Christ, including prayers like the Creed, among other prayers that have arisen by the need that the spirit has of claiming out to God).

Christians take their name from "Christ," who was crucified in the time of Pontius Pilate. They speak of a "Wise King" sentenced to death. (He who does not believe in the Holy Spirit cannot recognize, love the Father God or believe in Jesus and His mother. If one does not live in the will of God, then one is against Him and will not dwell in His Kingdom). "He, who is identified with the will of God, is God's son."

The Apostles, though physically the same individuals, underwent a spiritual transformation through the Holy Spirit. This spiritual awakening can be discerned in the stark contrast between their lives before and after the death and resurrection of Jesus (Acts 1:6-8, 2:1-4).

"The divinity and humanity of Jesus are inseparable." The Catholic doctrine teaches the confession of one God and one Son, our Lord Jesus Christ, perfect in both divinity and humanity. He is the true God and true man, with a consubstantial nature, sharing the same essence with the Father in divinity and sharing our humanity, similar to us in all aspects except sin.

In terms of divinity, He is born of the Father before all ages, serving as the Word and the promise of God. In terms of humanity, He is born of the Virgin Mary. He is the Christ, the Lord, the only begotten Son of God, a perfect union of two distinct yet inseparable natures. This union does not suppress the unique properties of each nature but preserves them, converging in one person and one subject. He is not divided into two persons but remains one, the Son and God. These beliefs have been transmitted to us by the prophets and Jesus Christ Himself, forming the foundation of our faith. After these things have been wholly regulated for us by Jesus, with all accuracy and harmony, "this one is Holy" (determined that no one is allowed to look for another belief or write it, adapt it, think it, or teach others).

"The world carries an origin dominated by demons, from the beginning they had the man "humanity" locked in the earthly existence and ignorance of their spiritual condition, and of a prisoner;" of offensive sins to God, which make us stay away from God.

(On the day of judgment for each of us, on that day, undoubtedly will be the discovery that the works of Jesus are true, in the sense of having been sent by God)!

NEW BIRTH

All those whose names are not written since the creation of the world in the book of life of the Slain Lamb; "Baptism".

By baptism, it refers to a rite of initiation or purification. Christian baptism consists of a specific application of water over a person, invoking the Trinity—the Father, the Son, and the Holy Spirit—in order to unite those who receive it with the resurrection of Jesus Christ. This constitutes the person as a Prophet, Priest, and King together with Christ, a son or daughter of God, and an heir of His kingdom. It integrates the baptized into the community of the Church as a living member of the mystical body of Christ, which was instituted by our Lord Jesus Christ for the forgiveness of Original Sin.

Baptism: The importance of being an antidote against original sin. (See Mark 1:1-11).

By belonging to Christ, the baptized person is incorporated into the Church as a member of the Holy people of God. Baptism liberates the person from the effects of original sin, introduces them to the new life in Christ, symbolically and effectively participates in Christ's death and resurrection, and redress them with the dignity of being a child of God. (See Romans 6:1-23 and John 3:3-7).

Baptism is administered to both adults and children, with the guarantee and commitment of the faith of their parents. This sacrament is administered by an ordained Minister or by a baptized person when an ordained minister is absent, especially in the event that a child is in danger of death. It requires consent from the parents or at least one of them or those who act as parents (tutors). "The desire of the righteous is always heard and granted by God because they only ask for good things and are pleasing to God."

Through baptism, we have died and been buried with Christ. Just as Christ was resurrected from the dead by the glory of the Father, we too will be resurrected from the dead and should walk in a new life. This circumcision of Christ is baptism. Upon receiving it, you are buried with Christ and raised because of your belief in God's power, which raised Christ from the dead. (See Colossians 2:11-15).

According to the Gospel, John the Baptist was aware that the ritual he was performing was an announcement for the one who was coming. Firstly, the announcement of John the Baptist was that "Jesus would baptize with the Holy Spirit" (See John 3:22-36).

The central element of the sacrament of baptism is water. It symbolizes regeneration to spiritual life because it is the source of natural life, signifying purification and new life. (Water is similar to and represents the essence of God: freshness, cleanliness, and purification.) The water used in the celebration of the sacrament must be blessed or consecrated during the ritual. The three valid modalities for administering baptism are immersion, pouring, and aspersion.

The Trinitarian formula is necessary, keeping in mind the words of Jesus: **"And baptize him in the name of the Father, and of the Son and of the Holy Spirit."** The sacrament should be administered using the Trinitarian formula.

The responsibility for choosing an appropriate name from Christianity, one worthy of a child of God, lies with the parents, godparents, and the Minister. Godparents are chosen to present the candidate and are committed to the Christian education of the one being baptized. To be a godfather or godmother, the minimum ageis 16 years old, and they must be Catholic, having received the first communion, and be married in the Catholic Church.

Any human being who has not received baptism can access it. If the person is an adult, they must express their desire to receive baptism, undergo necessary instruction about the faith, and fulfill the obligations through a catechism period (See Acts 8:36-38 and John 15:1-11).

The effects of the sacrament include the forgiveness of sins, including original sin and personal sins, the union with Christ through the sacramental character, the gift of the Holy Spirit, becoming an adoptive child of God, and integration as a member of the Catholic Church. Baptism is part of the plan of salvation, which also includes repentance, receiving the Holy Spirit, and dedicating one's life to God.

Baptism is an act performed with full awareness, symbolizing death to sin and resurrection to a new life in Christ.

Baptism of desire refers to those who wished to be baptized but passed away before it could be executed. These martyrs are considered baptized by their own free will.

Blood Baptism, or baptism of blood, implies the acceptance of death out of love for the Church or to defend a Christian virtue by an unbaptized person. This baptism occurs when a non-baptized person patiently endures a violent death for confessing the Christian faith or practicing Christian virtues.

Invisible Baptism is linked to Matthew 10:32-39, where those who confess their faith even at the cost of their lives receive the "baptism of blood." This baptism is effective when one is conformed to the passion of Christ and is coupled with the effects of penance and love for God under the inspiration of the Holy Spirit. **Whoever acknowledges me before men, I will also acknowledge him before my Father in heaven. But whoever disowns me before men, I will disown him before my Father in heaven. Anyone who loses his life for my sake and for the gospel will find it.** (Matthew 10:32-39)

The desire for baptism arises from faith, activated by the grace of God, initiating a process of interior sanctification guided by God's limitless power, leading individuals toward the sacraments (See Mark 10:33-45).

Regarding those in the past who lived before the establishment of baptism, those who, through no fault of their own, did not know or had no knowledge of the Gospel of Christ and His Church but sincerely sought God with a pure heart and tried to lead a morally upright life, they may also obtain salvation. (God knows everything and understands the intentions of each individual).

EXTREME UNCTION

Sacrament of the anointing of the sick, is administered to individuals who are ill or elderly, preparing them for their final encounter with God. This sacrament is based on the biblical reference from James 5:14-15: **(Is anyone among you sick? Let them call the elders of the church to pray over them and anoint them with oil in the name of the Lord. And the prayer offered in faith will make the sick person well; the Lord will raise them up. If they have sinned, they will be forgiven;** Extreme Unction highlights the importance of seeking healing for the sick and requesting the Holy Spirit's presence and comfort for them.

The illness of the body can sometimes be related to the evilness of the soul. However, it's important to note that the forgiveness of grave sins cannot be achieved solely through anointing or prayers; it requires repentance and confession to priests, who complement the sacrament of anointing.

The Sacrament of Extreme Unction, or Anointing of the Sick, serves a dual purpose: the forgiveness of sins and the alleviation of physical weakness in the patient. The primary focus is spiritual healing, with the body subordinate to this goal. This anointing complements the healing process initiated through penance, primarily aimed at the health of the soul, and, when appropriate, the body as well.

Extreme Unction also prepares individuals for the transition to eternal life. It contributes to reconciling us with the death and resurrection of Christ, similar to what baptism initiates. Baptism marks the beginning of our new life, while the sacraments of confirmation and communion strengthen us for the battles of our earthly life and the eternal one. Extreme Unction, administered to those nearing death, serves as a shield against the final spiritual battles with evil spirits. In this context, the significance of these sacraments becomes evident to the dying person, providing them with a greater chance of entering the House of God. It is typically administered to the dying along with the Eucharist, serving as spiritual provisions for their journey to the afterlife. Only presbytery priests are authorized to administer the sacrament of the sick.

The effect of spiritual healing is always realized through prayer, heartfelt repentance, confession, and participation in the communion of the Holy Eucharist. Physical healing occurs when it aligns with the patient's needs.

A unique gift of the Holy Spirit is the renewal of faith in God and the fortitude to resist temptations, including discouragement and despair resulting from sin. It's crucial to remember that forgiveness of sins requires genuine repentance and confession from the person receiving the sacrament. This sacrament bestows comfort, peace, and courage to overcome the challenges posed by illness or the frailty of old age.

Asking for the sacraments is crucial because, at the time of death, they are the only companions during the judgment. No one, not even parents, children, siblings, or any individual in person, can intervene on our behalf. What truly matters is the intention behind the work. Therefore, it is important to pray for the sick and for the souls of all those you know, as well as those you don't. In the case of someone who is approaching death, mutual prayer is especially meaningful.

BLOOD

Blood: Fluid that flows through the veins. Its main function is distribution and transportation of oxygen, carbon, etc. Blood is a fluid that continuously disperses.

Arterial and oxygenated blood are bright red, while venous and partially deoxygenated blood takes on a dark and opaque color. However, due to an optical effect caused by how light penetrates the skin, veins can appear blue. Like all tissues, blood is composed of cells.

The formed elements, also called figurative and articulated elements, are semisolid, which means they are half liquid and half solid, represented by cells and components derived from cells. These formed elements contribute to the blood's composition, forming the body, and everything in the body is composed of the same blood. The formed elements of the blood vary in size, structure, and function. Blood cells, including red and white corpuscles, travel through the blood to fulfill their roles in other tissues. They are the only blood components that perform their duties within the vascular space.

Red blood cells carry oxygen, hemoglobin, protein, etc., to the rest of the cells in the body. Hemoglobin, exclusively contained in red blood cells, is a pigment and a protein. Red blood cells also transport carbon dioxide, most of which is dissolved in the plasma or liquid blood and is extracted from the blood by the spleen, liver, and bone marrow. These cells have migratory capacity.

Blood is used as a vehicle to access different parts of the anatomy. White blood cells are responsible for picking up and destroying infectious agents and infected cells. They also secrete protective substances such as antibodies to fight infections.

Blood composition varies according to physiological conditions such as pregnancy, stress, sports, age, infection, cancer, etc.

Red blood cells may become stained palely by foreign substances like bacteria or external agents and others that enter the body during infections, contributing to inflammation.

White blood cells have a nucleus often covered by secretion granules. White cells, or white blood cells, increase in number during diseases, allergies, especially in viral infections, and conditions like cancer, which can lead to immunodeficiency and weakness.

A person's mood can also affect the entire body system if they are continuously under pressure, such as anguish, depression, anxiety, or constant sadness. "Living in sin is to be in constant anguish, and both lead to death."

Red blood cells are responsible for immunity and the secretion of antibodies, "substances that recognize bacteria." The antibodies bind with bacteria and destroy them.

Platelets serve to clot injuries that could affect blood vessels. In coagulation, platelets contribute to the formation of clots and are responsible for closing vascular wounds. Their function is to clot the blood. Platelets are the smallest cells in the blood, and a drop of blood contains about 250,000 platelets. When a circulatory vessel breaks, platelets surround the wound to reduce its size and prevent bleeding. Fibrinogen transforms into sticky threads and, with platelets, forms a net to catch the red blood cells that coagulate and then form a scab to prevent hemorrhage.

Plasma, or blood, contains water, proteins, hormones, electrolytes, glucose, amino acids, lipids, sodium, enzymes, antibodies, etc. Fibrinogen, globulin, and proteins are components formed in the liver. The properties of the blood flow are adapted to the blood vessels. The constant impulse is provided by the heart. An adult person has around 4-5 liters of blood. If a person with one blood type receives a blood transfusion with a different blood type, that person can become very ill and even die. (This is a reason for the institution of marriage.) (Genesis 20:24 and 1 Corinthians 6:16).

Blood is related to the elements that compose it, transporting oxygen in red blood cells from the lungs to the rest of the body. Likewise, blood transports nutrients in blood plasma, such as glucose, amino acids, lipids, and minerals, from the liver to the body, defending the body against infections from the digestive system. Blood also transports hormones.

Hormones, when released into the bloodstream, regulate the body's functions. Hormones regulate many functions in organisms, including mood, growth, tissue function, and metabolism. They act as a hormone communication network that responds to released stimuli.

Stimulants promote activity in tissues, and hormones are substances produced by cells in the endocrine glands. They function as messengers and are generally released directly into the bloodstream, where they have their effects on specific organs or tissues at a distance from where they were synthesized. They influence metabolism and spread throughout the body through the bloodstream, including the brain and heart. (The sin that produces anxiety makes the release of hormones harmful. In love, forgiveness, which is peace and serenity, changes the effects of these hormones to promote life and health).

VEGETARIANISM

Vegetarianism: Health, welfare, and purity; but also, the harmony between the body and the spirit.

Fatty acids omega3 is easier to obtain in a vegetarian diet, as found in various foods such as olive oil and nuts. A low level of nutrition can lead to cardiovascular diseases or mental illness.

In summary, if vegetarianism and any other diet are done improperly, it can cause anemia and deficiencies in vitamin Bcomplex, calcium, and proteins, among others. It can be very healthy and adequate if the diet includes various fruits, vegetables, legumes, cereals, B12-fortified foods, etc.

A vegetarian diet helps prevent coronary and cardiovascular diseases, as well as colon, ovary, breast, liver, and prostate cancer. Fruits and vegetables regulate body temperature, providing essential substances to the blood, which relaxes the organism and delights the mind, leading to total satisfaction of body, mind, and spirit by maintaining the balance of the molecular organism correctly and thus obtaining proper health and the prevention of diseases. These processes are related to absorption, digestion, metabolism, and elimination. Molecular methods are associated with balancing elements such as vitamins, minerals, amino acids, glucose, and conveyors of hormones, etc.

Nutrition is the study of the nutrients that make up the food. It is understood that after passing through a set of involuntary processes that occur after food ingestion, which is digestion; absorption, or the process of nutrients entering the bloodstream from the digestive tract, and their assimilation in the cells of the body.

Many common illnesses and their symptoms can often be prevented or relieved with good nutrition. Through nutritional science, we attempt to understand how and which specific aspects of nutrition influence health.

The body's metabolic reactions to nutrition involve natural compounds such as water, amino acids, proteins, vitamins, carbohydrates, fatty acids, natural liquids, fiber, etc. Suitable nutrition is the one that meets the needs of physical activity and the requirements for nutrients like vitamins and minerals. Hydration, especially with water and sufficient natural fibers, is also crucial.

The first documented nutritional experiment is found in the Bible, when King of Babylon captured Daniel and his friends. Selected as servants of the royal household, they were going to participate in the fine foods and wines of the King. However, they rejected it by preferring vegetables (legumes) and water under their Jewish dietary restrictions. The administrator of the King unconformity agreed to a study; Daniel and his friends received their food for ten days and were then compared with the King's men. By looking healthier than the others, they were allowed to continue with their nutritious vegetables' meals. (See Daniel 1: 8-16).

Oxidation: the dissolution of some foods is the source of body heat. Body fat can be synthesized from carbohydrates and proteins. Energy in blood glucose can be stored as fat or glycogen, adding milk and meat to the nutrition.

Calories, proteins, and minerals: there are six major types of nutrients that the body needs: carbohydrates, proteins, fats, vitamins, minerals, and water. It is important to consume these six nutrients daily to build and maintain healthy bodily functions. Additionally, most nutrients are involved in assimilation that carries them to the cells. Deficiency or excess of several nutrients affects hormone function, as nutrients significantly regulate the expression of genes in hormones; "in nutrition, our genes are expressed."

Ensuring growth and maintaining vital functions: poor nutrition could also cause oral health problems. When the body stops receiving the nutrients needed to renew tissues, the mouth becomes more susceptible to infections. Excess carbohydrates, starches, and sugars produce acids in the plaque, which adhere to dental enamel, causing its destruction.

At the base of the pyramid, the most significant area represents cereals or grains, especially whole grains, which constitute the basis of our diet. You will find vegetables and fruits in the middle of the pyramid, which helps us have more natural energy without side effects. To ensure that we get more than half of our calories from carbohydrates, it is necessary to consume the servings suggested in this group. Groups diminish in size as we move towards the pyramid's apex, as the number of foods represented in these groups is fewer for good health. The tip or apex of the pyramid represents the smallest group of foods, such as fats, oils, and sugars, that should be eaten in smaller quantities.

EXAMPLES OF CHANGES OF METABOLISM IN THE BODY

There are numerous examples of physical and metabolic changes that wisely occur in our bodies for our survival on Earth. At the same time, we come to acknowledge the wisdom of our Creator, God. For instance, the changes in a pregnant woman are designed to protect and nourish both her and the new life within her.

Pregnancy tests detect hormones produced as a result of metabolic changes, specifically hormones generated by the newly formed placenta. Blood and urine clinical tests confirm these bodily adaptations and manifest changes. These changes may manifest in altered perception of odors, fatigue, weakness, drowsiness, and, in some cases, increased energy in pregnant women.

These changes are not merely external; they have their origins within the body. The invisible becomes visible, in the same order that God shows Himself in the visible, letting us see His order with wisdom. (See John 1: 1-14).

Some changes can serve a dual function, being either beneficial or harmful. They are beneficial when they occur naturally and are necessary for the body's function. Harmful changes can be provoked or manipulated. Some effects even have scientific names, such as progesterone, a hormone that possesses sedative properties for humans, including strong tranquilizing and hypnotic effects.

Other noteworthy changes include disorders of the thyroid gland and anorexia, which can be visible effects caused by stress or anxiety. These effects are the body's way of manifesting distress. In women, stress or anxiety can lead to menstrual delays. It's common for individuals to develop aversion to alcoholic beverages and the smell of cigarette smoke, and this aversion can intensify in cases such as pregnancy or illness, as a manifestation of the body's response.

Progesterone is a hormone that relaxes natural smooth muscle, adapting to our physical needs. For men, this is useful in performing strenuous physical tasks, while for women, it aids in pregnancy. In some pregnant women, abdominal stretch marks may appear, as well as hyperpigmentation on the skin. In other cases, conditions like Chloasma on the face may develop. This hyperpigmentation can also occur due to the use of oral contraceptives, collagen diseases, or inadequate nutrition, all of which are manifestations of the body.

Inside our bodies, various hormonal effects are at play, facilitating adaptation to age, body weight, disease, or recovery.

from it. These adaptations are influenced by factors such as antibodies, estrogens, and progesterone (which activates milk production during lactation and contributes to uterine mucous repair, preparing the uterus for fertilization). These hormones also influence men, affecting both their physical appearance and character. However, excessive hormone levels can lead to adverse consequences, including weight gain, mental imbalances, physical ailments, moral and spiritual decadence, increased abdominal size, and conditions like ascites (excessive fluid accumulation in the abdomen).

Several factors increase the risk of a risky pregnancy in females aged 14 and over 35 years. These factors include drug, alcohol, and tobacco use, preexisting or pregnancyrelated illnesses, anemia, cardiovascular diseases, diabetes, hypertension, obesity, various infectious diseases, bleeding during the second half of pregnancy or in previous pregnancies, and body weight below 45 kg or over 90 kg.

Teenage pregnancy is a serious problem that often goes unaddressed and carries significant physical, moral, and social consequences. Adolescent pregnancies, involving young girls who are still in the developmental phase before reaching the age of twenty, pose complex challenges. These girls have not yet completed their full physical, moral, mental, and, to some extent, spiritual growth.

Teenage pregnancies can lead to severe repercussions for the wellbeing and overall development of both the young mothers and their babies. Pregnant teenagers are at risk of experiencing cephalopelvic disproportion, a condition arising from the incomplete development of their pelvic bones. This condition can potentially lead to anemia due to iron deficiency, as their blood levels may be lower than optimal.

Reducing sugar intake would be advisable due to its potential complications. Babies born weighing more than 4 kilos could lead to pelvic infections for their mothers during childbirth. These causes can be attributed to genetic factors and the type of daily nutrition that parents have been consuming and continue to consume regularly. Typically, children inherit these genetic complications and diseases such as obesity, diabetes, etc. from their parents.

The use of an Intrauterine Device (IUD) can reduce fertility and may cause various damages, including muscle abnormalities. Instead, we can turn to natural methods, recognizing that everything created by God is perfect, and there are no exceptions when it comes to procreation. We could consider using the method of tracking infertile days in women. "Pain saddens the spirit" (perturbation). (See Leviticus 15: 1-33).

Additional, less commonly acknowledged effects of alcoholism include the consistent consumption of beer, leading to an increase in the body's water content. When combined with a highsalt diet, this substantial influx of water and salt within the kidneys results in blood dilution, what would explain the cause of anemia and other illnesses. The heightened blood volume further leads to increased cardiac output, bronchodilation, an elevated respiratory rate, and the inevitable grease reservoir.

Metabolism, once again, represents the body's adaptive response to safeguard itself, resulting in heightened hormonal fluctuations. In cases of excessive fluid intake and frequent mood swings encompassing depression, acceleration, and aggressiveness, several physiological changes occur. These include an elevated heart rate, increased blood pressure, heightened venous resistance, potential nerve damage, imbalances in brain function, and a state of confusion that can ultimately lead to errors. (Refer to Romans 7: 14-25 and 8: 1-39 for further insight).

Another example of this disorder would be in an abortion, which is fatal physical harm to the mother and baby. In women, it will always have a moral effect, mental, spiritual, and psychological, as an imbalance in the body's function, they are in both notable acts.

In the presence of God, our intentions hold great significance; positive energy nourishes the spirit, while negative energy can taint our spiritual essence. The core of all essence resides within the presence of God, an unescapable truth. In His boundless mercy, a testament to His goodness and compassion, He bestowed upon us His Son, who offered us His transformative Church, illuminating the path to draw nearer to Him through the sacred sacraments.

HOMO SAPIENS

The human being: From the biological perspective, Homo Sapiens is an animal species, scientifically classified as such.

Homo sapiens, as a rational animal: It possesses the ability to transmit information, habits, imitation, and instruction.

The human organism: This is a wellorganized system encompassing the mind, understanding, consciousness, perception, emotion, memory, imagination, and will.

The age of puberty; the phase of ages varies according to the person. The changes are not marked by age but by internal hormonal development. Humanity should not be reduced to its sexual impulses, which sublimates or represses them. (Not everything is sex; it is necessary to know the times to praise God and develop our talents through meditation).

Women Continue to Live Long After Menopause: The human being's meaning goes beyond mere physical reproduction; it is a special being consecrated to God.

Puberty is always a development and a slow process in the human species. These bodily changes vary from one individual to another, adapting to the unique characteristics of each person. In addition to physical changes, it's imperative to emphasize that achieving balance also requires spiritual development.

Highlighted here are notable metabolic and physical changes in the human body. In the past, humans used to support the entire sole of the foot by bending it and distributing weight on the calcaneus. Nowadays, there has been a modification towards a lighter and more efficient walking posture. Furthermore, adjustments in the angle of the femur, the bone extending from the groin to the knee, have been incorporated into the body to enhance balance. The hip and pelvis have become stronger, shorter, and concave. The spinal column has transitioned from its former "C" shape to a more "S"-like configuration. These anatomical changes at the physical level are quite evident.

Human behavior has undergone significant transformation, with the most pivotal change being the evolution of the human mind. This evolution has given rise to creative ingenuity, empowering humanity to assert dominance over its environment.

Language serves as the cornerstone of all communication, drawing upon the interpretation of examples. Language is a natural tool employed by both humans and animals. However, it's crucial to recognize that language is a necessary conduit for the expression of the human spirit. The body serves as the vessel for the human essence, spirit, or soul, and sharing a human thought becomes impossible without the use of symbols and signs.

Human beings have long perceived themselves as distinct from other animals. This distinction, as outlined in Genesis 2:19-24, lies in the presence of an intangible entity known as the spirit, which serves as the locus for the manifestation of the human mind and personality.

"The spirit can exist independently of the body." Perhaps the most conspicuous display of human distinctiveness is the creation of art, which in turn shapes culture and mirrors the inner self through expression. Each individual leaves their unique imprint through actions, such as their choice of attire, vocabulary, moral and ethical principles, and the distinctive aspects of their personality. For instance, when scrutinizing a piece of artwork, a painting, their style of writing, their signature, or even their approach to crafting tools, it becomes possible to deduce the identity of the author, the architect, or the artist behind it. "Art stands as one of the most profound manifestations of human creativity and the expression of the spirit."

Nature generously bestows food upon us from the environment that surrounds us, prompting the development of our skills. Amidst the quest to enhance our comfort in the present, we must not lose sight of our spiritual origins. It's essential to recognize that our relentless pursuit of comfort might inadvertently impact on our genetic makeup, potentially affecting whether our descendants possess the fundamental traits necessary for survival in the natural world.

THE DREAM WITH THE SERPENT

I found myself in a dream, standing in a peaceful countryside village, but an atmosphere of terror hung in the air as people ran frantically. I tried to stop someone to understand the reason for their fear, but no one would pause to speak.

Finally, a man halted, glanced at me, and exclaimed, "Why aren't you running? Aren't you afraid of the beast? You should be terrified of being devoured by it!"

I was taken aback and asked, "What are you talking about? How can people fear an animal?"

He responded, a mix of fury and fear in his eyes, "Don't be naive; not even the entire world united could defeat the Dragon."

Before I could inquire further, he let out a scream of terror and tried to flee. I turned to see what had terrified him and beheld an enormous serpent approaching. Its head was the size of a bus and sported massive tusks.

The man looked back at me, as if urging me to run. And with regret on his face for stopping to warn me, the Serpent closed in, consuming people as it moved.

I stood frozen in horror, unable to run. It became apparent that the Serpent was not consuming people's flesh but devouring them whole.

Ahead, a group of people was fleeing, and the Serpent pursued them with relentless speed. In that moment, I mustered the will to react and dashed towards the nearby hills in search of a hiding spot.

I found refuge in a cave but heard voices inside. I called out to ask if anyone was there. A man emerged with an irate expression, sharply telling me, "There's no room here; find another place. Besides, this cave is only for relatives and acquaintances."

As he spoke, a monk dressed in a brown robe and a young man intervened. The monk said, "Why do you address her that way? Is she any different from us? She seeks shelter just like you and everyone else."

The irate man interjected, "We don't know her!"

The monk put an end to the argument, declaring, "Enough! She stays with us, and that's final."

The young man led me inside, where there were adults and children gathered around blazing bonfires, preparing food. He guided me to the campfire and introduced me to everyone.

Once I felt more at ease, I asked if anyone knew the origin of the colossal Serpent. With a hint of scorn, I added, "It's so horrifying; it seems like it escaped from hell."

All eyes turned to me, and one person remarked, "It did come from hell; it's the Dragon, the Serpent that has pursued us from the beginning."

Taken aback, I replied, "Isn't it supposed to be dead? That might explain its immense size; it must have been hidden all this time."

The monk responded, "It emerges from the darkness; it doesn't need to die."

We believed ourselves safe inside the cave when suddenly, a deafening noise shook us. We all stood still for a moment, and then we saw the Serpent sliding in front of the cave. I marveled at its length, wondering where it ended. Abruptly, it halted, and everyone shouted, "Run before it returns!"

The young man grabbed my hand, and we sprinted alongside the others. As we fled, the Serpent turned to pursue some of the people, and we were left terrified. We continued to run, leaving behind gruesome scenes of human flesh scattered everywhere, making the earth appear drenched in blood.

We approached a range of mountains, uncertain of our location and where to seek refuge. Suddenly, a man emerged from the tall grass, looking like he was standing guard. With his hands raised to show he meant no harm, he signaled to us and called out, "Don't worry; I have no intention of harming you. I belong to a group that inhabits these mountains!"

We cautiously observed him, ready to flee at the slightest sign of danger. From his position, he beckoned to some of the people that were with him, saying, "A few of you come forward so they can see I'm telling the truth.

Five people approached him, followed by a larger group. As we drew near, the young man asked, "How is it that all of you are alive? How have you managed to escape?"

He answered, "No, we haven't escaped; the Serpent hasn't reached this area yet. It won't be long before it detects us and arrives."

I inquired, "What's your plan when it arrives? Do you have a strategy to confront or evade it?"

As we continued along a descending path into the heart of the mountains, he replied, "We have no plan, for we don't need one. We have something more important to do, and you all are fortunate to have arrived at this moment."

As we followed the winding path, we came upon a remarkable sight: a large gathering of people situated within a circular border nestled in the heart of the mountains. This border formed an oval shape, and the individuals within exuded an aura of tranquility and serenity. Their interactions were filled with love, greetings, and blessings, transcending language barriers and encompassing diverse backgrounds – people of all languages, traditions, religions, rich and poor, preachers, pastors, young and purehearted, virgins of varying ages, and women whose dedication to their families earned them the title of saints. Among them were those who had repented with sincere hearts, their past transgressions transformed into precious gold. The common thread among them all was that each person possessed a Bible written in their own language, and their demeanor reflected a deep reverence for the teachings inscribed within. They shared a collective commitment to seek and discover the truths that God had in store for them.

I approached this gathering, but one young man singled me out and urged me to draw closer. He approached me with a palpable sense of excitement and passion, akin to a profound love. He exclaimed, "You don't seem as thrilled as you should be! The momentous day has arrived!"

Feeling a bit shy and unsure of the cause for his jubilation, I responded, "Truthfully, I've stumbled upon this place by chance. I'm not certain I should be among you all. If you would permit me, I'll step aside and wait until your celebration concludes."

The young man chuckled briefly but maintained his fervor as he replied, "Don't say you're here by mere chance. Look around – there are people from every corner of the world, of all ages. Each one of us has been touched and saved by the grace of God, just like you. No one has arrived here coincidentally, and certainly not by chance. At noon, when the sun is directly above that ridge, the Son of God will descend to uplift His people regarding the Serpent and to encourage us not to despair. Moreover, it's time to select someone from among us, to be guided by Jesus, to save us from the Serpent."

Hearing this, I became apprehensive about being in the midst of such an important assembly. However, a sense of hope welled up within me as I contemplated the prospect of someone being chosen to confront and defeat the colossal Serpent that had been terrorizing everyone.

I confided in the young man, "In that case, I think I'll keep my distance from the group. Once the chosen person is identified, could you kindly point it out to me?"

He responded earnestly, "No, stay here. Perhaps you might be chosen. The Lord looks not upon physical appearances but upon the hearts, and He alone knows them."

His words left me feeling humbled and somewhat intimidated. As I was lost in thought, the sun began to cast its brilliance upon the very edge of the mountain where the multitude had gathered. A light more radiant than the sun descended from the sky, settling upon the ridge. This radiant light gradually concentrated at the edge and began to consume itself inwardly. As the light dissipated, the figure of Lord Jesus emerged, seated upon what resembled a throne. He began to speak, "I am the Good Shepherd who leads His sheep along the path of truth and light, for I am the light."

A profound silence enveloped the assembly as all listened intently and reverently. People strained to absorb every word, yearning to glean the wisdom and guidance that Jesus would impart. They thirsted for His words as if parched souls seeking water to quench their spiritual thirst, eager to store this divine wisdom in their hearts, knowing it would sustain them in the days to come.

Suddenly, a hush fell upon the gathering as Jesus rose from His seat, a vision of indescribable beauty – more resplendent than the sun, more captivating than the most precious gems. His eyes radiated an unparalleled brilliance, and His skin glowed with an ethereal luminescence. His feet gleamed like pure gold, His robe was immaculate white, and His hair was as soft as a baby's. Witnessing this, I felt a profound sense of awe, as if I might faint, yet I remained steadfast. Jesus's presence filled me with strength, and His voice was like a gentle, soothing stream – a balm for body and soul. His words flowed through my ears, caressed my skin, permeated my mind, and reached deep into my heart, infusing both body and spirit with vitality. I observed the same transformative effect on those around me; they trembled and rejoiced, their beings enveloped by the life-giving power of His words.

Once the young man saw Lord Jesus on His feet, ready to choose, he became excited and whispered to me, "The moment of choosing has arrived. Can you imagine? He will pick the one to fight against the serpent!" As Jesus uttered a name, the young man was shocked, and he stared at me in disbelief. I, too, was taken aback and asked him urgently, "Has He already chosen? Who is it? I want to see!"

I turned my gaze to Jesus, searching for any sign of His choice. To my astonishment, Jesus was looking directly at me. I glanced around, thinking there must be someone else, but I found no one. I looked back at the young man and said, "That's impossible! You must be mistaken. There are priests, pastors, brave individuals, and virgins among us. Any of them would be more suited for this task than I."

But Jesus responded calmly and assuredly, "I am not mistaken."

I continued to plead, "Please, Lord, choose someone more prepared and worthy than me. Here are others who are more deserving." However, Jesus simply said, "Save my saints."

As He was saying this, suddenly a humming noise was heard like of an earthquake, and right away everyone knew that the Serpent had found us. Shortly after, the Serpent crossed the cliffs and devoured a group of people given into prayer.

Embarrassed, I got closer to Jesus and said: "Lord, forgive me for your Saints, I have already failed right from the beginning, but there's still time for you to find someone else who will not fail you like me".

"I am not mistaken, and they will not move if you don't ask them, and those who have been devoured don't worry about them. These people are already safe!"

As the Serpent continued its relentless assault, devouring nearly half of the gathered assembly, I felt an overwhelming sense of urgency. Without hesitation, I raised my voice, urgently pleading with those who remained: "Flee for your lives! Stay close to God and do not waver!" My impassioned cry spurred them into action, and in frantic desperation, they scattered in various directions to escape the Serpent's grasp.

However, my plea did not go unnoticed by the malevolent Serpent. In response to my desperate call, it swiftly pivoted its monstrous form toward me, its predatory intent palpable. At that moment, terror coursed through my veins, and I braced myself for what seemed an inevitable demise. The Serpent bore down upon me with alarming speed, its head looming menacingly just inches away from me. With deliberate malevolence, it began to sway from side to side, revealing its formidable fangs in a sinister display of intimidation. Its forked tongue slithered menacingly near my face, as if taunting me with the impending threat.

Yet, amidst this harrowing confrontation, I clung to a profound faith that Jesus, our protector, was present and would shield us from harm.

In that dire moment, my eyes were fixed on Jesus, who turned His gaze solemnly toward the malevolent Serpent. As if provoked by an unrelenting arrogance, the Serpent dared to address the Son of God Himself, its voice dripping with disdain: "Behold, the Son of God, as I feast upon your beloved Saints! You watch helplessly, for their hearts are drawn to me in love." Despite the Serpent's audacious taunt, Jesus remained steadfast, His countenance unwavering, and His divine presence exuding a sense of unwavering authority.

Amidst this tense confrontation, Jesus maintained a calm and penetrating gaze, His eyes seemingly reaching into the depths of my soul. I stood there, my heart pounding with suspense, unsure of what action the Lord would command me to take, or whether the Serpent would strike at any moment. Paralyzed by terror, I longed to flee, yet my body remained unresponsive. In the midst of this unsettling standoff, a remarkable revelation began to unfold before my eyes: the Serpent, despite its malevolence and hunger for destruction, refrained from even inadvertently encroaching upon the area where Jesus stood. It glided smoothly and deliberately, its predatory eyes fixed on the countenance of Jesus, who, resolute and undaunted, did not yield to the Serpent's taunts or threats.

As the Serpent continued its menacing dance, Jesus began to utter words that resonated with the sacred verses of the Bible: "He who is willing to sacrifice his life for the Gospel, for My sake, will find salvation. Whoever confesses Me before others, I will acknowledge in the presence of My Father in Heaven."

These words penetrated deep into my heart, revealing their profound meaning. I comprehended that Jesus was referring to those who had succumbed to the Serpent's relentless assault. In their final moments, these brave souls did not waver in their devotion to the one true God or His sacred teachings as conveyed in the Holy Bible. Their unwavering faith was evident in their eyes, which shone with an otherworldly passion, as if they had already transcended their mortal bodies and were poised to ascend to the divine presence of God Himself. With this understanding, fear and apprehension dissipated from my being, for it became clear that the Serpent's ruthless consumption of these souls yielded it no victory.

Amidst this nightmarish scene, a group of men, accompanied by their wives, children, and teenagers, confronted the Serpent in a desperate bid to appease its fury. They offered their service, pledging to provide the Serpent with whatever it desired. They even presented axes and knives as potential offerings, hoping to stave off its wrath.

The Serpent, with its head held high, remained eerily silent as it listened to their pleas. But gradually, an infernal rage seemed to consume it. In an explosive burst of violence, it mercilessly devoured the innocent children and teenagers before their anguished parents' eyes. The Serpent then encircled the remaining men, its intent to intimidate them palpable. Despite their efforts to maintain an appearance of courage, one of the men succumbed to overwhelming fear, trembling and weeping uncontrollably. At that very moment, the Serpent seized the opportunity to devour their helpless wives.

The men, driven by a mixture of despair and anger, turned accusing eyes toward the one who had cried out in fear. Without hesitation, they brutally killed him with the very weapons they had intended to offer. In a gruesome tableau of loyalty and submission, they knelt before the Serpent, brandishing their bloodstained weapons as symbols of unwavering fealty. A sinister gleam of satisfaction glinted in the Serpent's eyes as it unleashed another violent frenzy, consuming these devoted but misguided souls. It was only then that the Serpent redirected its malevolent gaze back toward Jesus, who remained undaunted and resolute.

As Jesus continued to speak, revealing the true nature of the beast and its insidious hold over the people, saying: "At the beginning, they heard said, he who does not worship the beast and its image or put its mark, the beast will kill him. I said to them that whoever kneels has already lost his life, all this time and they did not understand anything". A profound understanding began to dawn within me. I comprehended that the beast was, in fact, sin itself, and those who succumbed to its allure were unwittingly worshipping this malevolent force. Such individuals were already spiritually dead, destined for a dark and desolate realm.

Turning to me with a sense of urgency, Jesus implored me to save His people from the clutches of the Serpent's deathly grip. My initial response was one of fear and doubt. I felt wholly inadequate for such a monumental task, pleading with Him to find someone more capable.

In that intense moment, Jesus fixed His gaze upon me, his eyes filled with solemn determination. He assured me, with unwavering conviction, that He was not mistaken in choosing me for this crucial mission. Overwhelmed by the weight of His trust, I conceded, vowing to follow His guidance closely.

Meanwhile, the Serpent continued its relentless onslaught, devouring all who ventured too close, including those seeking solace near Jesus. It remained impervious to any threat, growing increasingly wrathful. Then, with lightning speed, it locked onto me as its next target. Panic surged through me, and I desperately sought refuge beside Jesus, reluctant to touch Him. The Serpent advanced rapidly, consuming everyone who, like me, had sought solace near the Lord. Its malevolent gaze remained locked onto Jesus, who, in the face of this imminent danger, continued to radiate an aura of unshakable tranquility and serenity. With a measured calm, Jesus averted His gaze from the Serpent and addressed me directly.

As I stood there, witnessing the unyielding determination in the eyes of Jesus and realizing that even in His presence, lives were being consumed by the relentless Serpent, fear welled up within me. With a trembling voice, I implored the Lord, "Lord, if you wish me to save your people, I beseech you to shield me from the Serpent's grasp. Let my life be preserved, and I shall know that your presence guides me."

With a gaze filled with boundless love, Jesus granted my plea. His eyes sparkled with compassion as He assured me, "Yes, I grant you this, live and rescue my people." The Serpent, seething with fury, drew ever closer, and in my desperation, I turned to Jesus, urgently asking, "Tell me, Lord, what must I do? Where should I go to evade the Serpent's deadly reach?"

With serene authority, He directed me, "Go to the holy land, beyond its borders, the Serpent cannot enter. Gather all my saints and protect them. Now, I must depart."

Desiring further reassurance, I inquired, "Lord, when shall I see you again? How will I know that I am on the right path, fulfilling your divine will with your approval?"

In response, He conveyed, "I am the morning's star, the beacon that guides the world. I shall return to be with all, and my radiant light will shine for the entire world to witness. In that time, we shall be reunited, and you will be assured of my presence."

With a sense of profound significance, Jesus began to move slowly, eventually halting before His radiant throne. A resplendent bluish light emanated from His being, intensifying into an almost blinding whiteness, rendering it impossible to behold. This brilliance gradually ascended, giving way to the emergence of a mysterious dimensional portal, through which the radiant light began to vanish.

After Jesus departed, my sole focus became escaping the relentless pursuit of the Serpent, which now bore a furious grudge against me. With unwavering determination, I sprinted from the mountains and arrived at a nearby village crowned by an imposing church atop a hill. This grand church resembled a palace, and its towering cross gracing the rooftop could be seen from every corner of the village. My heart swelled with joy, for I believed that within those sacred walls, I would find refuge from the Serpent, remembering Jesus's promise that the Serpent could not enter the Holy Land.

While rushing towards the church, I encountered another young man who was also fleeing from the Serpent's menace. Overcome by exhaustion, I briefly halted on the road, ready to resign myself to a grim fate. Observing my distress, the young man swiftly returned and urged me, "What are you doing? Why are you giving up now, so close to safety? Come on, get up!"

Wearied and despondent, I replied, "No, go, save yourself, hurry, it's almost upon us. Don't let yourself be devoured on my account!"

With unwavering determination, he countered, "If you won't save yourself, then I'll stay here, and the Serpent can devour us both. I can't live with the knowledge that I left you behind to perish without lifting a finger to help. I don't think I could bear that burden."

In that moment, I recognized that Jesus was speaking to me through this compassionate stranger. I praised Him silently in my heart, for I remembered Jesus's assurance that I would not be consumed by the Serpent. I smiled and replied to the young man,

"You don't understand how much your words mean. I see the love of God in your heart. Let's go."

Together, we raced towards safety, with the Serpent relentlessly closing in on us. We entered the grand church and knelt before the altar, beneath a crucifix bearing the image of the crucified Christ. As we prayed fervently, I felt a gentle touch on my shoulder and heard my name spoken. Startled, my entire being quaked with emotion when I recognized the voice-it was Felix, standing before me. I couldn't speak or move, overwhelmed by the shock of seeing him here. Felix called my name once more, his surprise evident, "What are you doing here? How did you find me? Did you know I was here? Who told you?"

Gradually regaining my composure, I managed to respond, "I had no knowledge of your presence here. Tell me, have you been searching for me?"

He replied, "No, I'm here fleeing from the Serpent. Haven't you seen it?"

As we conversed, a chill ran down our spines as we noticed the Serpent outside, peering through a window. The young man, now beside us, placed his hands on our shoulders and spoke softly, "Forgive me for interrupting, but have either of you considered what we should do? I can't even think straight in this situation."

Turning to him, I explained, "Jesus told me that the Serpent cannot enter the Holy Land. Let's stick together and see what unfolds." I had scarcely finished when the Serpent shattered the church's door and entered, its malevolent gaze fixed upon us. It proceeded to desecrate the church's altar. In a frantic search for escape, I spotted a staircase leading to the upper floors and whispered to both, "Quick, this way, let's go, hurry!" Together, we ascended floor by floor until we reached the church's attic.

From the small attic window, we watched in dread as the Serpent deftly maneuvered in and out through the large windows on each floor of the church, relentlessly closing in on us. We also had a vantage point to see a cemetery behind the church, where frightened people sought refuge among the tombstones. The Serpent detected their presence, sensing their scent, and with sinuous grace, it slithered toward them. It extended its body to reach and devour them while keeping us trapped inside the church, ensuring our escape remained impossible.

Observing this dire situation, the young man by my side couldn't contain his distress as he asked, "What did Jesus mean when He mentioned the 'holy land'? Didn't you see how the Serpent entered the church and ravaged the altar? You witnessed it tear those who sought refuge in the cemetery to shreds. Are we in the wrong place?"

Feeling helpless, I replied, "I don't know. I fear it's too late to ascertain that now. Escaping seems impossible." We had reached the pinnacle of the church's attic, and the Serpent was already winding its way through the massive structure, inching closer to us.

A wave of sorrow washed over me, though Felix, trying to conceal his own apprehension, couldn't quite fathom the depth of my despair. I began to bid them farewell, expressing gratitude for having known them. I thanked the young man for the invaluable-

lesson of resilience he had imparted to me, and I thanked God for him. To Felix, I expressed my appreciation for employing me when I needed a job and said my farewells.

Suddenly, the young man peered out of the attic window and exclaimed, "God is merciful! We still have somewhere to run. Look at the size of the church's cross!"

I inquired, "Yes, but what can we do? What's your plan?"

With a determined glint in his eye, the young man responded, "Let's climb the cross. Perhaps the Serpent won't reach us there, and we can save ourselves. At the very least, we'll have the privilege of facing death on the cross. What greater honor could there be than to share the same fate as Jesus?"

Motivated by the young man's idea, Felix and I decided to climb the cross. I ascended first and reached the top, followed closely by the young man. Felix, however, met a tragic fate as he attempted to make his way out of the window. The Serpent, with its massive fangs, reached him and fatally pierced his body, witnessed by the young man and me. The young man prayed earnestly for Felix, entreating God to welcome him into heaven, and continued his prayers in a hushed tone.

Embraced by the cross's apex, the young man and I clung to it as the Serpent tore through the attic's roof and emerged, closing in on the young man. He watched in shock as the Serpent's fangs punctured his body, and immediately, he began to pray, commending his spirit to God. He expressed gratitude to God for sparing his life and for the love he had experienced. With his final words, he confessed, "God, I wish I could have loved you more, but forgive me, for I loved you with all that I am." Then, he passed away.

I stood there, paralyzed and alone. Escape was impossible, and I began to plead and cry out, "Lord Jesus, you promised me that the Serpent would not take my life! Where are you? Why have you abandoned me?" As I uttered these words, the Serpent's fangs pierced my body, penetrating my stomach and one of my legs. I felt the warmth of my own blood covering me. My spirit then separated from my body and began to ascend toward my head. Through my spiritual eyes, I witnessed my lifeless body as it withered away.

I felt as though I had a new existence, an unfathomable dimension opened before me. In the distance, a brilliant light shone, and I could discern numerous people moving about within it. As the radiant light drew nearer, it walked through the figures without disruption, gradually taking on the form of a man. It completed its transformation as it approached me and spoke, saying, "I told you that in the Holy Land, it cannot enter. Here, it holds no power. Now, come, for the people await you; the celebration of my saints is unending."

The radiant figure extended a hand, and I took it willingly, realizing that I was leaving my earthly body behind like a discarded garment, its purpose fulfilled in helping me grasp the mysteries of God. Now, I found myself adorned in a new garment, white, pure, and eternal, standing beside the Saints and Jesus himself.

THE DEVIL'S REVELATION

On another occasion, I was preparing to sleep, and as soon as I lay down on the bed, an intense sleep overcame me. It forced me to remain in bed involuntarily, much like previous instances. This deep slumber was far from voluntary, and it tormented me greatly. I constantly sought ways to escape this condition, but all my attempts were in vain. Being trapped in this dream filled me with anxiety, yet I tried to calm myself, knowing that I had to face whatever awaited me. Despite my fear of the unknown, the grip of sleep was relentless, leaving me no choice but to confront it head-on. In my desperation, I turned to prayer to fortify myself morally, fully aware that my physical abilities were of no use.

Suddenly, a mocking, masculine voice echoed: "So, you're willing to confront me."

For a moment, I entertained the thought that an intruder had entered my room and was hiding, which sent a shiver down my spine. Nevertheless, I summoned courage and declared, "Coward! Why don't you reveal yourself? Come out from your hiding place!"

I desired to rise from my bed, but an oppressive heaviness held my body in place. The voice continued to taunt me with laughter, saying, "You wanted to see me."

He drew closer, his dark and malevolent presence looming over me, and I came face to face with him. The sight was unfathomable; before me sat a demon, and a chill of terror gripped every fiber of my being. It felt as though my bones were desiccating within me. Desperately, I tried to steady myself with slow, deliberate breaths, struggling to regain composure. I finally mustered the courage to inquire, "What is it that you seek from me? Why have you chosen to unveil yourself in my presence? Am I of such significance that you would deign to manifest before me?"

He said: "I come to ask you to give up already, don't fight for your life anymore. regardless, in a few days, I will come for you; you belong to me".

I replied: "You have said it. It is my life. I have the right to fight for it, and if you are going to take me, you'll have to wait for those days. I won't give up!"

The demon countered, "Very well, but it will avail you of nothing. However, I could offer you something. You could prolong your existence, provided you perform certain services on my behalf. You see, I have matters requiring resolution, and I require individuals for this purpose."

Curious, I inquired, "Such as? Look at me! How could I be of any use to you? Don't you require someone capable of attracting attention?"

The demon explained, "I can bestow upon you certain abilities; all you need to do is accept. Those who serve me gain access to my power, and the wisdom of this world becomes theirs. Without me, they are nothing!"

I retorted, "I see now. You wish to use me to draw others to you, to make them serve you."

The demon confirmed, "Exactly. I already have many in my service, but those who worship me receive even greater power— the power to discern the depths of others' souls and the art of passion."

Curiosity piqued, I asked, "Could it be that Felix is one of your followers?"

The demon's irritation was palpable, and he nearly erupted with fury. He seethed, "Don't mention him to me! I detest him."

Pressing further, I inquired, "With all your power, do you hate a mere mortal like him? Could he be superior to you? What makes him so repulsive to you?"

The demon's rage subsided momentarily, and he reluctantly revealed, "Fine, I'll tell you. Nevertheless, no one will believe you, and your time is limited. Knowing this won't benefit you. I hate him because he is not one of us. I sent many of my minions to ensnare him, but he defeated them all. Recently, we tried to break his spirit, hoping he would succumb to despair and turn to hatred, thereby worshiping me. I nearly had him, but he eluded my grasp."

I followed up with, "So, what transpired with Felix and his brother; was it your doing?"

He responded, "Yes! I also laid Felix's heart bare in the presence of his brother. I will corrupt him until he worships me!"

And then, I woke up.

REASON FOR COMING TO THE USA

I left Mexico because the father of my child was an extremely aggressive person. He consistently threatened me with his work firearm, aiming it at both my head and my child's. He subjected us to frequent physical abuse and unrelenting verbal humiliation. He even went so far as to lock us in our house, threatening to kill my son and me if I confided in anyone.

My situation was further complicated by the fact that he held a position of authority as the regional commander. At the time, I was just eighteen years old, and my son was only one year and three months old. We seized the first opportunity to escape. I spent a few days hiding with my family and acquaintances, but living in fear and secrecy was an unbearable prospect. Sadly, my family couldn't offer me any protection, and I feared for their safety.

Another significant reason for leaving was that my family didn't see anything wrong with underage marriages. In some families, it's customary for parents to relinquish responsibility once their children become independent. For these reasons, I made the difficult decision to escape to this country.

Amidst the turmoil, I sought solace in prayer, earnestly beseeching God for guidance. Through the conduit of dreams, He conveyed a message to me - that I would depart from the country and find healing for the emotional scars inflicted by that man.

Leaving the country had to be done in secret, even from my family, with the exception of my sister Ana, who knew just in case something happened to me along the way, allowing her to locate me.

I received a message from the person organizing our journey, indicating that the next trip would be in fifteen days. To my surprise, only seven days had passed when I received another message, announcing our departure the following day. This abrupt change filled me with anxiety, but I had no other viable options, so we embarked on our journey toward the border.

Our journey began on foot through the desert. We walked for nearly two weeks, enduring treacherous terrain, scorching daytime heat, and freezing nights. The weight of our provisions, my concern for my child, and the haunting howls of coyotes made it an arduous and profoundly unsettling experience.

Once we crossed the desert, we continued our journey by car and bus, passing through numerous cities. This phase of the trip lasted for a month and a half, providing me with ample time for reflection.

Personally, arriving in this country felt like a fresh start. I was faced with freedom to choose my path, good or bad, knowing that the outcome would shape the rest of my life. Each moment, I held onto the belief that God had allowed this journey to happen, guiding me towards a purpose I had yet to discover.

After an extended period of travel, we finally reached New York City. Upon our arrival in NY, I contacted my cousin who lived in Elizabeth, NJ, asking him to pick us up.

I stayed with my cousin and his family in Elizabeth, NJ for some time. On one occasion, I attempted to travel to the state of Wisconsin, where my father resided. However, as I prepared to board the bus, an overwhelming sensation overcame me, paralyzing me with uncertainty. This intuition revealed the presence of something significant waiting for me, compelling me to investigate further.

As time passed, I continued my search without a clear direction or a sense of what I should be looking for. I only held onto the belief that something would guide me when the time was right..

My cousin and his boss, who worked as a truck driver distributing Mexican products across New Jersey, occasionally invited my son and me to join them, allowing us to explore different cities. One day, we visited the town of New Brunswick, and as I stepped out of the truck, that same perception washed over me once more, though with less intensity than before. I knew then that my search would begin here, in the city of New Brunswick.

I relocated to New Brunswick, NJ, hoping to uncover the reason behind this persistent perception. However, after living there for about three weeks, doubts crept in, and I began to question whether I had made a mistake. The disappointment was overwhelming, and I found myself in tears, pleading with God for a clear sign that would dispel my doubts and confirm that I was not chasing an illusion.

That very night, I had a dream, and I focused intently on the preceding scene to understand its significance. In the dream, I heard a woman's voice, prompting me to walk towards its source. I found myself in a vast room with rows of seats and no doors. In the room stood a majestic lady with a serene and dignified presence. Her countenance radiated purity and grace, despite her long, elegantly adorned garment.

She spoke to me, saying, "I've been waiting for you. Why don't you come and see me?" She appeared somewhat saddened.

I responded, "I'm sorry, do I know you? Please tell me your name, maybe that will help me remember." It was at that moment that I realized she was the Virgin Mary. Right away, I began to reproach her for what had transpired in Mexico. In an instant she showed me vivid images of the terrible misfortunes and evils from which she had protected me. My anger gave way to sorrow as I acknowledged the truth of her words. I finally asked her, "Why didn't you prevent all my misfortunes?"

She began to explain: "I have protected you in the bitterest moments of your life. I am with those who suffer the misfortunes, not with those who commit them, and from these misfortunes, I have protected you."

Then, after feeling remorse for my earlier complaints, I asked her, "Why are you sad?" I suspected it was because of my lack of devotion.

She replied, "I cannot leave this place, so you will have to come in and see me."

I looked more closely and noticed that her feet did not touch the floor, which left me deeply impressed.

When I awoke, I felt a profound sense of regret and remorse because I believed the Virgin was also sad because I had not been attending Holy Mass regularly. However, now I felt a deep commitment to seeking her out, especially after she had allowed me to glimpse that sacred place.

After waking up, I diligently searched for this place, and to my astonishment, I found it—the Church of Nuestra Señora Del Carmen in New Brunswick, NJ. As I entered, the first thing I saw was an image of the Virgin of Guadalupe. I prayed to apologize for my previous neglect and promised her that I would faithfully attend Holy Mass from that point forward.

As I stood there, more people began to arrive for the Holy Mass, and I involuntarily found myself moving in a circular motion to make room for them. Without realizing it, I ended up in the exact spot I had seen in my dream. Overcome with emotion, my legs trembled to the point of almost giving way.

Internally, I thought, "No one will ever believe this extraordinary experience I'm having." The emotions overwhelmed me, and tears streamed from my eyes. A young woman nearby noticed my tears and stopped to embrace me, offering comfort, unaware that my tears were tears of joy.

As time went by, I found myself in various living situations, each fraught with its own set of challenges. In the first place I lived, constant fights between the couple were a regular occurrence, and the situation escalated to the point where the woman even stabbed her husband due to their excessive alcohol consumption. This compelled me to seek another place to live.

My second residence proved no better, as I discovered that some of the occupants were involved in drug use. Feeling uncomfortable and unsafe, I decided to move once again.

On the third attempt, I believed I had finally found a peaceful place to reside. A seemingly respectable family occupied the house, consisting of the housekeeper, his pregnant wife, their two year old son, an uncle, and the housekeeper's cousin. They all appeared respectful and kind. However, after a few months, the housekeeper's brother and sister-in-law came to visit, and the brother's behavior towards me was unsettling. He sat uncomfortably close, making unwarranted advances and displaying a clear attraction to me, despite not knowing me. This situation left me feeling extremely uneasy, especially because he seemed unconcerned about his wife's presence. I excused myself and retreated to my room to avoid the discomfort.

A week later, they returned with the news that they would be moving into the house permanently. During their first week in the house, the brother forcibly separated from his wife. He engaged in daily arguments with her, escalating to physical abuse, which

I could hear from my room, leaving me terrified. Ultimately, he threw her out of the house. She did not press charges because of her love for him and the fact that he was the father of her two children. She hoped for a reconciliation.

After ridding himself of his wife, he confessed to me that he had done it to be with me, a revelation that caught me completely off guard because I had given him no reason to believe I reciprocated his feelings. Having witnessed his behavior, I felt nothing but fear towards him and consistently rejected his advances.

On one distressing occasion, he attempted to assault me, forcefully trying to enter my room and restraining me by holding my hands tightly. He uttered threatening words, stating that if I didn't comply willingly, he would resort to force. My child was asleep at the time, and I screamed in hopes that someone in the house would hear me. He callously laughed, claiming that there was no one else in the house to help me. In that moment of despair, my child emerged from his room, brandishing a broom to defend me. He struck the man on the head, causing the aggressor to momentarily hesitate and reconsider his actions. I was left in suspense and fear, uncertain if the man would harm my child or proceed to assault me in front of him. Eventually, he decided against any further action and slowly retreated towards the exit, threatening that his humiliation would not go unanswered before finally departing. Internally, I fervently invoked God, thanking Him and my child for the brave act that deterred the man from carrying out his intentions.

The following day, my child and I went out in search of a new place to live. However, we returned to the house later in the afternoon because my child had fallen asleep late in the day. I had entrusted him to the care of the housekeeper's wife, whom I paid to look after my child while I worked. On this particular occasion, I left my child with her as I went out to buy dinner. Upon my return, I was met with a cruel act of revenge by the individual who had previously tried to assault me. He had handed my child over to the police, falsely claiming that someone had abandoned the child in the backyard of his house.

In a state of desperation, I immediately set out to search for my child. The police launched an investigation, and the man was subsequently arrested. My child and I were placed under the protection of the New Jersey Division of Youth and Family Services (NJ DYFS).

Initially, a gentleman was assigned to assist me at DYFS, but he was later replaced by a woman to ensure my comfort and confidence, reflecting their good intentions. The social worker presented my case in court, where a judge would ultimately decide our fate.

The judge advised me to pursue my education and offered assistance in caring for my child while she sought a better situation for both of us. She specified that I should continue my studies, including learning English and completing my basic school education.

I began studying for an hour a day while simultaneously holding two jobs—one in the morning at a clothing packing company and the other in the evening at a restaurant. After four months, I returned to court to provide an update, and to my surprise, the judge informed me that she would be returning my child to me within the same week. This decision marked a turning point in our journey.

A year had elapsed since I arrived in this country, and I was growing increasingly desperate. In my prayers, I beseeched God to send me a sign, an angelic presence, to reassure me that He still acknowledged and considered my journey. This hope was what kept me anchored, sustaining my belief that I would eventually discover my purpose.

Coincidentally, during this time, a young man named Rami had also been fervently praying to God. He sought a connection with someone who shared his devotion to God, a person who could serve as a beacon of faith and remind him that God always listened to his prayers.

After a few days, Rami confided in me, revealing that he had been making the same request just moments before our paths crossed. I will forever be grateful to God for introducing me to Rami, as through him, I came to understand the profound nature of true friendship. It dawned on me that friendship should not only be practiced with friends but also with family, parents, siblings, and, above all, with God.

Rami was a young man of deep faith, one who feared the slightest offense against God and loved Him so profoundly that he longed to be in His presence in heaven. It was for these qualities that he was often seen as an earthly angel. When I met Rami, he was in the final year of his college education. After graduation, he returned to his home country, where he held immense love for his parents, cherishing the blessing of being raised by two parents who shared his profound faith in God.

I extend my gratitude to Rami for his exemplary devotion to prayer, his unwavering faith in God, and his immense respect for his fellow human beings, especially his siblings. Rami's life was a testament to the power of faith, love, and friendship, and I feel truly blessed to have known him.

A challenging period arrived when I lost both of my jobs, leaving me with no money even to provide for my child's basic needs. It was during this desperate time that I encountered a woman and humbly asked for her assistance. She welcomed me into her home to care for her newborn child, offering me modest compensation and meals. However, these resources were insufficient to cover my essential expenses, and I had already accumulated two months' worth of rent arrears in my previous residence.

This kind woman mentioned that she knew of a gentleman who was genuinely goodhearted and could potentially help me find employment. She expressed confidence that I would be okay if I took up a job offer from him. Curious about the nature of this work, I inquired, and she revealed that it was at a bar.

I deliberated on this decision for several days, but the desperate cries of my child for food became too much to bear, and I found myself without any means to provide for him. It broke my heart to witness his hunger, and I was on the verge of despair. With the guidance of this compassionate woman, I made the difficult choice to work at the bar for a brief period, hoping that it would only be a temporary solution until I received a call back from one of the numerous job applications I had submitted. In my prayers, I asked God to ensure that His will be done.

One morning, I had a dream of a young man who resembled the spirit I had encountered in a previous dream when I was a child. In this dream, he had a physical form, and as we stood face to face, he spoke to me, saying, "I'm waiting for you; the time has come, get ready!" I asked him where he was, and he replied, "I've always been with you."

Seeking more clarity, I inquired further, "I mean, if you're among mortals, perhaps you're already born, and we will see each other again as you promised. Has the time come?"

He responded with a reassuring smile, "Yes."

Filled with excitement, I asked, "How will we find each other, and how will I recognize you?"

He replied, "You will know it; I'm waiting for you."

Then, I awoke from the dream. I had always considered these visions to be mere dreams, unsure of their significance or if they would ever materialize. However, this particular dream left me more unsettled than usual. If it were to come true, as previous dreams had, it would signify the moment I had been eagerly anticipating—the revelation of my purpose, the reason for my existence.

That evening, as the woman introduced me to a man named Felix at the place where I was to work, his very first words to me were, "I'm waiting for you!" From that moment forward, I was determined to delve deeper into his heart, ensuring he was indeed the person from my dream, all the while praying to the Lord for guidance to confirm my intuition.

I soon discovered that Felix possessed a remarkable gift: unwavering faith in prayer to God. He exhibited great patience through his profound meditation on life's circumstances, exemplifying waiting with unwavering confidence that if he acted righteously, God would heed his prayers. I observed him setting aside time for prayer and reflection before making decisions in challenging situations.

CAUSE OF MY DEATH

Reflecting on all the distressing moments I had endured would fill me with sadness, yet it never pushed me to the brink of madness. Observing my occasional bouts of sorrow and discouragement, the social worker seized an opportunity to prescribe medication for depression, never bothering to mention the potentially severe side effects. Over time, I came to realize that she was repeating this pattern with most of her clients. It dawned on me that her motives weren't driven by genuine concern for my wellbeing but rather by personal gain and professional credit.

As I found myself sinking into despair, unable to extricate myself from the clutches of these pills, I deeply regretted ever crossing paths with this woman. The most distressing aspect was the threats she leveled at me, including the prospect of taking me to court and separating me from my child should I dare to cease taking the medication.

During the course of my medication, I grappled with sluggish digestion, persistent heartburn, and excruciating pain that bred frustration, despondency, and sleep disturbances. My sleep patterns oscillated between excessive slumber and restless nights. Ingesting the pills seemed to submerge me in a sea of discomfort, eventually leading to obesity. It later became clear that it was due to swelling and fluid retention, which caused my weight to balloon from 115 pounds to 185.

When I voiced my grievances about the physical toll, the social worker pledged to assist me. She arranged a visit to a doctor who prescribed even more pills, often at higher dosages for depression, along with supplementary ones for sleep and digestion. This resulted in a total daily intake of up to eight pills, initially divided into two doses and later increased to three.

Refusing to comply with this overwhelming regimen led to the social worker's dire ultimatum: she threatened to take legal action to separate me from my son and even discussed deportation if I dared to resist. To ensure compliance, she personally supervised my morning medication routine.

Over time, attempting to halt the medication became an exercise in futility as it triggered unbearable and overwhelming anxiety. I shared my suspicions of addiction with the social worker, citing my concerns backed by advice from parents and teachers, but she vehemently denied any such possibility. The pills wreaked havoc on my body, causing nosebleeds, chronic nasal dryness, and intermittent pain. Initially dismissing these as mere consequences of the weather or allergies, I soon found the bleeding intensifying after a few weeks.

Gradually, the pain escalated to the point of tears, and these discomforts began to impede my daily life. Bleeding extended to my gums, accompanied by a strange sensation of a salty fluid originating from my head and coursing through my face, ultimately seeping through my gums. Initially, it resembled white foam, then turned yellow, and eventually became tinged with blood. As the days unfolded, the bleeding intensified, causing tooth sensitivity, frequent pain, ulceration, inflammation, and even bleeding from my lips.

On one occasion, Felix pointed out a red stain on my face, prompting me to rush to the bathroom and examine it in the mirror. It resembled a bloodstain, leaving me puzzled about its origin, yet I didn't dwell on it too much at the time. A few days later, while I was in my room applying makeup for work, I was startled to find tears of blood welling up in my eyes. When I mentioned this to the social worker during her visit that same afternoon, she dismissively laughed and assured me that it was a normal side effect of the pills.

As time passed, I began to notice alarming changes in my health. I frequently found myself sighing, and my stomach was plagued by persistent, sometimes excruciating pain that occasionally led to vomiting. I also experienced chest pressure and pain, prompting frequent coughing spells. It slowly dawned on me that these ailments were a direct consequence of the medication the social worker had introduced me to, under the guise of it being essential for my wellbeing. She assured me that many people in the country underwent similar treatments and that there was nothing to be concerned about. At that point in my life, I was still quite young, having recently turned twentyone, and I remained oblivious to the lengths she would go to for her own pride, as I didn't truly know her.

One Thursday at the beginning of the month, I unexpectedly began to bleed, even though it wasn't the time for my regular menstruation. I shared this concern with the social worker, who reassured me that irregularities in menstruation were to be expected due to the medication. She claimed it was a common occurrence among her clients and advised me not to worry. However, my physical condition deteriorated rapidly. I grew pale, felt dizzy, nauseous, and weak. My alarm heightened when I realized the bleeding was unusual, resembling pure blood as if it were flowing from a ruptured vein. I could tell by its light, bright color, and it lacked the typical odor of menstruation. It was an experience I had never encountered before, and I was unsure of the potential consequences. Therefore, I decided to see a doctor on Monday morning.

Strangely, by midday on Sunday, the bleeding had ceased, but my dizziness, nausea, and weakness persisted, along with the persistent paleness of my face. I tried not to worry, convincing myself that with better nourishment, I would recover.

A hemorrhage: That Sunday morning, I had a peculiar dream. In the dream, I found myself dressed as a bride, surrounded by unfamiliar people busily preparing floral arrangements, tables, and my wedding dress. The dream filled me with nervous excitement, and all my senses were focused on the emotions, making it almost feel real. I searched for my family among the crowd but couldn't find them. I asked the woman helping me with the wedding dress about their absence, and she replied, "Don't worry; perhaps they will arrive soon, or maybe they are already in the chapel. It's best if you concentrate; we're twenty minutes late." Her demeanor and actions struck me as eerily familiar, resembling those of the social worker.

As the dream continued, I eventually stood before the altar in the chapel, with the guests following behind me and the groom waiting. When I approached him, he turned and, with a stern expression, remarked, "You're twenty minutes late!"

Gradually, I began to wake up, holding the image of the groom's face in my memory. He was a complete stranger, and the dream left me unsettled due to the intense emotions I experienced and the absence of anyone I knew, except for the woman whose-behavior had resembled the social worker's, provoking a sense of fear.

On that particular Sunday, while I was at work, I began to notice some troubling symptoms. It felt as though I were suffocating, unable to breathe properly, as if my body was deprived of oxygen. Despite the freezing weather due to the snow, I rushed outside for a breath of fresh air. Strangely, I couldn't sense the cold, and this realization frightened me to the point of tears. Desperately, I prayed, asking God to grant me even a hint of the chilly breeze on my face. I plucked a few green pine leaves from a nearby garden, crushed them with my nails, and tried to inhale their scent, although it wasn't easy. Crying, I beseeched God, and almost instantly, a sense of calm washed over me. I attributed this serenity to my prayers. Once again, I cried, but this time it was tears of joy, as I began to feel the cool air and the aroma of those pine leaves, a moment I'll never forget. Filled with gratitude and thanking God in my heart, I returned to work.

Later in the day, anxiety crept in, and I assumed it was because I had missed my medication time. I took my pills, and they brought temporary relief. However, a few hours later, the anxiety returned, the same relentless anxiety induced by the pills, growing in intensity and becoming unbearable. It was accompanied by stomach pain, leg pressure, headaches, and an all-encompassing chill. I rushed to the bathroom, where I cried and screamed in pain. After a few minutes, the pain subsided and eventually vanished. Since I was in a public place, I had to compose myself, wash my face, and reapply makeup. I believe no one heard my cries due to the music playing in the background, and I returned to my duties.

After another two hours, the same overpowering and uncontrollable anxiety resurfaced, even before the usual time for taking my prescribed medication. It was the same anxiety that had haunted me as the doctor's recommended time for medication approached. In desperation, I decided to take two more pills to alleviate the torment. An hour later, the pain returned, but this time it coincided with the scheduled time for taking the doctor-prescribed medication, so I ingested that as well. By the end of that night, I had consumed far more medication than was prescribed. I refrained from seeking help at the hospital because I feared nobody would believe the severity of my distress, as I experienced moments of temporary stability.

A regular customer, who frequently visited the establishment, approached me, exchanged greetings, and inquired about my family. The mere thought of my family overwhelmed me, and I burst into tears. I quickly apologized and retreated. I tried repeatedly to regain my composure, but something peculiar happened; my tears continued to flow uncontrollably. When I glanced at the clock, I realized it was time to close up and head home. This gave me a glimmer of hope, thinking that perhaps I would feel better the next day. If not, I resolved to seek medical attention, as I would be outside work hours and responsibilities.

That Sunday, as I headed home, I found myself emotionally sensitive, and tears still streamed down my face. Upon reaching home, I apologized to Felix and retreated to my room. As usual, Felix waited until he saw the light in my window and received my signal that all was well. However, this time I refrained from turning on the light because the illumination from the staircase hurt my eyes, which I attributed to exhaustion.

While ascending the stairs, I experienced dizziness and tingling sensations in my legs. It was evident to me how my nerves seemed to misalign in my hands. Then, suddenly, an unusual sensation overcame me, and it felt as though my spirit detached, leaving my body up to the level of my knees. I found myself in a state akin to a waking dream, unable to believe what was unfolding before my eyes. Despite this extraordinary experience, I remained on my feet, observing it all in disbelief.

At that moment, I checked my pulse in my feet, which had progressed up to my knees, and in my hands, which had reached my elbows. I also experienced chest pressure and an uncontrollable urge to sigh. I resisted the urge with all my might, but it felt as if my life depended on that sigh, filling me with immense fear. I screamed and shouted loudly for help. I needed assistance desperately. Although I heard people talking in their rooms inside the house, no one came out to my aid.

I called out to Felix, urging him to help me as I felt increasingly unwell and strange. He asked me to return to my room, and I could sense the confusion in his demeanor. Perhaps he suspected that I had secretly consumed alcohol at work or that I was creating a scene for attention, assuming that my recollections of family were affecting me. He contemplated these conclusions while my remaining minutes of life ticked away.

I was unwilling to wait for them to believe me, so I decided to walk to the hospital, as it was nearby. While crossing the street, I felt my spirit rise to my stomach once more, causing my legs to collapse, and I fell. I prayed to God, desperately asking for the dignity of reaching the hospital before my life ended. I mustered a bit of strength and ran, determined to arrive in time.

As I passed a bridge about three or four blocks from the hospital, my spirit rose to my stomach again, and I fell to my knees once more. This time, the impact on my knee was even harder than before, but I had lost sensation in my legs, and the pain was absent. It intensified my fear.

Once more, I beseeched God to allow me to fulfill my final wish. My vision grew dim, and it became increasingly difficult to breathe. I could hear someone calling my name from a distance, but no matter how hard I tried, I couldn't focus my sight. Then, I cried out to God once more, and suddenly, my perception returned. I saw Felix by my side with the door of his truck open, shouting my name and urging me to get in.

When I could finally see and respond to him, it brought relief, but I initially hesitated to accept his help. However, he insisted, so I got into the truck. We drove a couple of streets and reached Robert Wood Johnson Hospital. For me, that short distance felt eternal because I began to sense that someone or something was pursuing me, causing fear and drawing closer. At times, I glimpsed a dark shadow shifting from side to side, moving toward me.

Near the entrance of the hospital, my vision darkened once more, and I struggled to see. My breath grew shallower, and I couldn't stand or walk. I implored Felix to guide me to the hospital entrance for assistance, all while an overwhelming fear enveloped me.

When my vision returned, I entered the hospital and pleaded for help, but nobody believed that I was dying. They asked me to sit on a bench and wait. I sat down, but I couldn't wait, as I knew I had only a few minutes left to live; I could sense it diminishing.

My vision darkened again, and the pulses in my arms and legs faded away. Nerves writhed, inflicting intense pain, and I began to agonize. I asked Felix to intervene, and he managed to bring some doctors over, but I could only perceive them briefly. At that point, a young man arrived with a wheelchair, inquiring if I needed it. I complained since the pain had become unbearable, and my abdomen had started to harden, and my insides felt as if they were dying. My pulse fluctuated, slowing down and suddenly racing, as it struggled to stabilize, exacerbating my suffocation. With great effort, I tried to explain how terrible I felt.

They transported me to a section where they instructed me to change into a hospital gown. However, changing was difficult due to the pain, and one of the nurses helped me, her expression betraying doubt about my condition. She asked if I had consumed alcohol or if I was seeking attention. Struggling to speak, I informed her that I was dying, but she dismissed it as pretense. I insisted that I was not pretending, but she asked for details on what I felt or saw that made me think I was dying. I explained that I was convulsing, and I felt my spirit attempting to leave my body. She responded that we had no spirit, we simply died, and everything shut off like sleep without dreams.

I became irritated and asked her, "How many times have you died?"

Her response was curt, "None, or I wouldn't be here!"

I retorted, "Exactly. So, you don't understand the pain I'm going through."

She said, "We have no spirit; we're no different from animals."

I shot back, "You probably have children, so why do we have them if they're just meant to live like animals?"

By then, they were already helping me back onto the stretcher.

The nurse appeared irritated with me, and from what little I could perceive, I overheard her telling others that I was losing my sanity.

IN THE LINE OF DEATH

By this point, I was already slipping into consciousness, overwhelmed by the excruciating pain and torment. The last thing I could discern was the doctors placing instruments on my body to monitor my fading pulse. With a perplexed gesture, they turned to Felix, seeking answers about my condition. I could no longer endure the agony; my vision dimmed once more, and I couldn't help but cease my cries. They made numerous attempts to administer the serum to my hands and feet, but my veins proved elusive, exacerbated by the violent convulsions wracking my body. Eventually, after several attempts, they succeeded. The pain was so excruciating and intense that I felt my nerves tearing, losing all control over my movements.

Out of nowhere, a chilling, ominous shadow loomed over me, settling upon my form. To my utter dismay, my bones seemed to wither, and my tongue adhered to the roof of my mouth! The agony was so excruciating that my exhausted body could do nothing but tremble in terror, engulfed by an overwhelming, unutterable anguish that robbed me of the ability to scream!

I was attempting to defend myself from the dark shadow within me, but its visage was already before me! It enveloped me with its dark cloak, which is the abyss of darkness, and my very being traversed a thread that emitted such a deafening sound it wounded my temple. It resembled a thin silver string, yet it possessed an intense and acute quality, as though it marked the boundary between life and death.

At that precise moment, the initiation of my retrospective work began. My memory unfurled, and I began to perceive my entire life in intricate detail, including all that I had heard and spoken. My memory gathered every joy, sorrow, physical and moral pain, caress, love, and hatred—absolutely everything. My spirit was acutely aware of this comprehensive recollection.

I experienced immense joy for the good deeds I had performed but also endured intense pain for my faults. Since my conception, I had been cognizant that I was merely passing through this world. During my retrospective work, I discerned that even in my childhood, the dark shadow had attempted to make me aware of its existence through various manifestations. This included witnessing the deaths of others and confronting physical and moral pain, demonstrating that death indeed exists and is a stark reality. However, I could not grasp its full significance at that time.

As he guided me through the darkness, I encountered a pain akin to the very essence of death itself. It was the same agonizing sensation that those who had passed on had felt, and it was a pain that humanity, in its entirety, would eventually come to know. Moreover, during this journey, I was acutely aware of the suffering of those souls who had not yet seen the light of day. Their anguished cries and pleas for divine justice reverberated around me.

For most of them, their physical forms were not fully developed, yet their complete spirits lay dormant within their mothers' wombs, awaiting the moment when they could love the beings who had bestowed upon them the gift of life, eager to explore the creations of their Creator, God. It dawned on me, with a heavy heart, that abortion was not merely the termination of a physical body; it was the expulsion of a soul, stripping it of the same fundamental right we all possess: the right to life.

My torment and sorrow began, and what I was about to experience defied description, for it was only the beginning of a profound and inexplicable journey into the depths of my emotions.

While I was on the other side, the dark shadow spoke to me with an assertive tone: "Address me as father, for I am the one who has begotten you."

Terrified, I couldn't discern the identity of the speaker. Yet, he persisted, repeating his words, and I resisted by asserting that I already had a father.

He retorted, "I have been your father from the very beginning."

He revealed to me a profound lineage, from my physical father's spirit to the earliest spirit he had conceived with his dark essence. He showed me how he had been entwined in the spirits of my ancestors, coursing through generations in my blood and spirit. With an incredible and almost unbearable speed, he transported me back through time going back to the first woman! where I found myself within the inner thoughts of a woman. I couldn't see her face, only her inner world, as if I were inhabiting her body. She was aware that she wasn't alone and contemplated the man she was wed to. However, the presence of another man before her was alluring, nearly hypnotic. He spoke to her, telling her to let herself be carried away by what she was feeling and that no one would ever find out. He started touching her, and she became unconscious; he overwhelmed her with caresses, and they started committing a sexual act. As she began to open her eyes, a thought raced through her mind: "It's not true that I will die. I'm not dead, nothing has happened to me!" But swiftly, a growing unease overcame her, manifesting as dizziness and discomfort.

I witnessed that a part of that man had become incorporated into her, though she remained unaware of it. It appeared as a dark stain, an enduring shadow of some sort. This man had an eternal origin, originating from God, for God is the creator of all. However, this man's intentions and actions were starkly opposed to God's will. It was that dark spirit within him that set him apart, driving him to act against God's divine purpose. After this revelation, I was returned to my own being.

During this journey, I beheld all of humanity tainted by this shadow, slowly corroding the pure white spirits. It was as if this shadow possessed a life of its own, distinct from God's essence, and it embodied everything that stood in opposition to God's will and actions. God had initially separated it from Himself, for He found it abhorrent. However, it had persisted and continued to exist, sustained by us and extending its influence over every being, gradually infiltrating what belonged to God. Throughout all of this, God remained steadfast in defending what had always been His.

In that moment, I also came to a profound understanding of what is often referred to as "The Original Sin." My moral anguish intensified as I grappled with the realization that after this life, we would transition to a different reality entirely, one that was distinct from the existence I had known. Throughout my earthly life, I had occasionally harbored doubts, even considering these beliefs to be mere myths, tools to govern human behavior and curb crime. However, it was in that moment that I confronted the overwhelming truth that far exceeded any fiction I had encountered before.

By that point, it was abundantly clear to me that this was not a mere fabrication; it was an undeniable reality. It was in that moment of revelation that I grasped the profound purpose of the individual known as Jesus, who was, in fact, the Son of God, and the significance of His sacrifice. He had to offer Himself with a pure body, blood, and spirit for His sacrifice to hold meaning and validity. Through this sacrifice, He redeemed and purchased our souls, infusing them with divine radiance through the workings of the Holy Spirit, all with the ultimate aim of returning them to God.

As I descended further into the abyss, a profound realization gripped me. I recalled the times when, in good health and life, I had begun to doubt the existence of any afterlife, dismissing it as a mere human invention. In that moment of reckoning, I felt profound remorse and began to implore forgiveness. However, it was a journey into the depths of darkness, led by death itself, on the form of a shadowy figure with a humanlike appearance, that I was now undertaking.

As we descended deeper, an agonizing sensation enveloped my spirit, akin to an unquenchable fire. I felt an unbearable thirst, not for any worldly pleasure, but a thirst for the compassion and grace of God. I finally understood it - a thirst that could not be sated by anything in the material world, and it intensified my anxiety. This thirst was born from sin and the fiery passions that flare within us, from the fury and hatred that can consume us, to the passionate fire ignited during sexual acts, and even the satisfaction derived from causing harm to others.

In this state, disordered passions inflict pain, sprout in burning, burning and torment upon the soul, it enfolds the soul as in the physical burning multiply in moral pain. But unlike physical fire, this burning does not consume, nor does it bring an end to the soul's suffering. Here, everything is eternal, including the agony of despair and anguish, knowing that one will never again witness the divine light symbolizing God's presence and losing that presence forever. I was acutely aware of having committed these sins and deserving the punishment they brought.

"My faults were in me as if I were committing all of them at once, and thus I suffered from all of them simultaneously. My mouth dried up, and it pained me greatly for having vilified it with all the bad words I uttered in life. I felt as if I had many insects crawling in my legs, but there were none to be seen when I looked. It was merely a sensation, a torment stemming from my lack of control over my body, from dishonoring it. Each part of my body endured suffering commensurate with the magnitude of my transgressions. My eyes bore etchings of malevolent intentions, while my ears endured a cacophonous buzzing like raucous machinery. There was also a slow, everexpanding acute resonance, the result of having heeded everything except for the things of God. All of this served as my torment, which was provoking me to clamor for repentance.

My spiritual body was corroded with black darkness up to the chest. I was naked and felt ashamed. It wasn't solely due to my spirit; it was more because all my faults had been exposed, and this intensified my moral pain, making it unbearable. The form of my spiritual body mirrored my physical body, but without any physical exaggerations.

I realized that it wasn't enough to merely possess the sacraments; their value lies in living them out, defending them, and being faithful to them. The sacraments are a means to become children of God. It involves acting as a child of God and striving for holiness. Furthermore, it means always proclaiming God.

I had been there for only an instant, and I couldn't endure it any longer. Moreover, an unbearable smell permeated the place, causing intense discomfort. Initially, I couldn't identify the source; it was reminiscent of being immersed in ammonia. Then, it dawned on me that this place was death, and I found myself here because of my transgressions. Death embodied all forms of impurity, with each sin emitting its distinctive stench. It reeked of putridity, akin to festering sores oozing with decay, and the odor of sexual impurity, it was unbearable! It also carried the scent of decomposing human flesh afflicted by disease. Everything within this realm was heightened to an extreme, making it stifling and insufferable.

The spiritual essence of those still living on Earth was overwhelmingly present in this dimension, tainted by their sins. The essence of earthly spirits reached the realm of death, bearing an indescribable essence. Their sins set them apart individually, etching marks upon their spirits. Sin itself is death. (I believe this was akin to the mark carried by Cain for his sin—initially of hatred and ultimately resulting in murder). The torment intensified as I realized I could no longer take any action to alert or offer hope to those still living, for where I found myself, there was no escape.

Suddenly, an external fear gripped me, distinct from the fear I already felt from witnessing death. It was akin to observing an enormous meteorite hurtling towards Earth, knowing it would bring utter destruction to everything and everyone. This new fear was approaching me, amplifying my existing dread. Emerging from the shadows roughly three meters away from me, an immense demon materialized, sending tremors through my entire being. I recognized it; it was the same one that had foretold my death three weeks earlier. Panic overwhelmed me, and I desperately wanted to escape, yet the sheer terror of facing it rendered me immobile. I attempted to shield my face, avoiding its gaze. At that moment, I recalled that such beings were real, as described in the Holy Bible, and my disbelief transformed into remorse. Internally, I lamented, "If I had believed, even out of fear of them, I wouldn't have committed sins." Then, I considered the world, filled with people unaware of the truth, and realized that others would inevitably witness the same horrors, each according to their spiritual state. Who was I to possess a spirit when others did not? I pondered: "Am I favored, or was it an injustice for me to have a spirit?"

The demon, visibly agitated, interrupted my thoughts, began to shout an acute hurtful scream. It commenced as a menacing roar, transitioning into a blend of barking and prolonged squealing—an agonizing cry of beastly discord that threatened to shatter my being. The unbearable sound resonated throughout the surroundings, seemingly omnipresent, regardless of distance, for time held no sway in that realm. I felt defeated, fearing it would rush towards me or drag me to the fires I had yet to witness. Until that moment, I had not encountered a burning inferno, and I assumed it might be what awaited me.

However, I noticed that the demon remained stationary, its countenance betraying a peculiar mixture of delight and despair, as if it sought to intensify my torment. Yet, something held it back. Its gaze shifted upwards, and I looked for what he was looking at. A faint, radiant light began to pierce the darkness, its brilliance dwarfing the sun's radiance by thousands of times. This light was directed towards me. I experienced an overwhelming fear, different from the terror I had known before—an inexorable and excruciating reverence that washed over me. The demon emitted a bellow and retreated, bowing its head in reverence. I was profoundly awed. I discerned that the light was none other than God, the Almighty Father—the Creator of Heaven, Earth, and the Universe. Even in death, His creation remained intact, just as in life. His throne was resplendent and undiminished by the magnitude of His creation. His immense power left me trembling in awe.

Embarrassed, I bowed my head, and within myself, I thought, "Lord, I am unworthy of your presence, but I can no longer bear being here."

Then, the demon shouted, though his lips didn't move, and his voice resounded solely through his will: "She belongs to me!"

In my conscious thoughts, I protested, "No, Lord, no!"

He insisted, "She committed me, and she must repay what she received from me."

In my defense, resolute because I had always ensured not to entertain any offers from the demon as much as I could, I countered, "No, I owe you nothing. I have never asked you for anything!"

He took my spirit back in time to a period of financial prosperity when I was even offered gifts and generous tips. He claimed, "It was me who provided those for you, because of me, you had what you desired. You owe me, and now you must pay."

I responded firmly: "I have already paid through my hard work. I never made any pacts or agreements with you, and if you gave me anything, it was of your own accord. I now understand that your role is to tempt humans and awaken ambitions in them, but what I received was never intended to serve you." Hearing this, he grew furious, realizing he could do nothing.

Despite the complex emotions I experienced after what I had witnessed, I couldn't help but feel furious with myself for not having been stronger against the temptations. At the same time, a deep sadness enveloped me as I thought about the innocent people who were now lost in a haze of fleeting pleasures, completely unaware of the spiritual consequences. It was in that moment that I truly grasped the spiritual meaning of perdition – being hypnotized, not knowing what one is doing, and living in a state of unconsciousness.

I was terror-stricken by the demon's mocking gestures, fully aware of the excruciating suffering I was enduring. The unbearable torment was so overwhelming that I longed to die again so that I wouldn't have to see it ever again. I felt suffocated to the brink of fainting, overwhelmed by its noxious stench.

Suddenly, a crevice opened in the abyss , revealing a flame that emitted deafening lamentations filled with great suffering and horror, which began to afflict my being. Within these flames were spirits already being consumed by their sins, restlessly shifting from one place to another. As they drew near to one another, their flames intensified, and their lamentations of suffering multiplied exponentially. Just when I thought I could endure no more, I witnessed the arrival of another demonic figure. This creature had the appearance of a dogman with long, thin ears pointing upwards. Its skin was dry and highly flexible, while its eyes gleamed with contempt and malevolence. With its claws, it swiftly ascended the crevice of the abyss, displaying remarkable speed, agility, and flexibility in its entire body. Once the demon had fully emerged, the crevice sealed shut again, leaving me awestruck. It became apparent that these entities could venture from Hell to the realm of death to torment newcomers.

I fell into despair and cried out to God because, at that time, I could already see through the light as if it were a window to the dimension of God. I saw the Saints who were around the throne of the Lord, though they were distant and barely perceptible. They appeared as humanlike forms but were spirits enveloped in the light of God. Despite God being the primary focus, He embraced everything. The Saints moved and conversed with each other, radiating peace, love, and harmony, even though they were distinguishable from a great distance. It was an indescribable sight. I understood that the flash of light reaching me was also healing me. I had an unending desire to be among them, yet sadness overwhelmed me because my faults were preventing it.

I clamored to the Lord, saying: "Lord, I deserve all this punishment for offending your purity. I regret my offenses for eternity, for I acknowledge the greatness of your power, whether to save or punish me. It pains me deeply that I doubted your existence in life, believing the words of those who claimed You didn't exist. But now, it is too late. Lord, I acknowledge my deserving of this punishment, but I implore You, please, I don't want to go. I didn't truly know You. Forgive me!"

The light of God was visible in the distance, yet it was both unbearable and awe-inspiring. It held a greater allure than water due to the excruciating thirst inflicted by the realm of death.

He told me: "Don't claim that you didn't know Me."

Right at that instant, He revealed to me my mother's affection and purity, the desires for righteousness in her spirit, and how it had been passed down through generations so that I, too, would inherit it.

He said, "I am the one who gives life and the love that resides within them. Humanity exists because of the love that dwells within them, and I am love."

In my defense, I added: "Yes, Lord, now I understand, but it's too late. How could I have followed Your example when there wasn't a single person close to me who could help me understand who You are?"

I also remembered that when I was a child, I heard people say that whatever you ask the Saints in prayers, they would grant it to you, and right at this moment, I had all the Saints available to me. I spoke to them, saying: "You who are with the Lord, and through your compassion towards those who do not know God, please intercede for me. I beg you, do not allow my ignorance to condemn me. Have mercy on me, for I can no longer bear being here. I don't want to stay here any longer!"

A woman with a maternal essence in her voice replied: "We can no longer do anything for you."

A nobleman, with the dignity of his being, answered: "I left many examples and many books."

Another one said: "I left examples in the family that God granted me. We do not have any power to save you or to condemn you; we already did what we had to do, and that is why we're here".

I understood that everything was true. I had no more to say, and I began to clamor for all those who were still alive because I was already at the moment of being sentenced, waiting for God's decision. I said to God, in prayer, "Lord, Lord!"

He replied: "You know that not everyone who says 'Lord, Lord' can enter the Heavenly kingdom because here there is no place for impurity."

"With great sadness, I came to understand more about His infinite love for me and every human being, without exception, because we first originated from Him, from the spirit, and then from the flesh. I grasped that He loved me but not the impurity within me, for He is righteous, and my punishment was fair.

While He was showing me images of the holiness of my grandparents and other people who followed and obeyed the goodness in their hearts, I kept crying out, 'Lord, Lord,' in a sense of desperation. I felt ashamed to be in the presence of God and all those who were pure and heavenly. My humiliation intensified when I realized that many more would find themselves in the same situation as I, and I would be powerless to help them. My opportunity had ended, my life was meaningless, as well as my death!

"I began to apologize to the entire world - to my mother for the pain she endured during my birth, for dedicating her life and youth to imparting moral education to me. To my father for his unwavering dedication and love, which I had squandered. I also sought forgiveness for any instances in which my attitude had set a bad example due to my blindness and lack of love for God. I implored the Lord to take everything into my account.

God then inquired: 'What do you have to say about them?' He revealed the spirits of all those I had clashed with in the last years leading up to my death.

In that moment, tormented by my presence there, I beseeched God, saying: 'Lord, do not judge their actions as sins, especially those directed against me. Instead, grant them understanding of You, so they may come to know You. Lord, You have the power to do all things, send someone who can help them understand and, if possible, save them. Please, do not let them condemn themselves because of me. And, if it serves any purpose, I forgive them!

Repentant for my weakness in not resisting evil with all my might, I confessed to God: 'Lord, I fell into the vices of impurity, but I did not know You. I am sorry, and I love You!'

He responded: 'See how much you loved Me.' He showed me images of how I praised Him during the Mass ceremony. However, upon leaving, I would quickly revert to harboring bitterness and resentment against those who had conflicts with me. I had never truly embraced forgiveness, and God's presence would depart from me."

He added: "I could not support or dwell in a heart like that."

I couldn't deny it before God; He showed me the truth with all the details.

As my chances seemed to slip away, the demon leaped for joy, eagerly anticipating that God would deliver me into its power.

Desperate, I implored God, saying: "It is true, but please, do not allow this one to draw any closer to me. I have also been good, and from my childhood, I have loved You deeply. I have always prayed to You, asking You never to abandon me. You could have taken my life before I had the chance to condemn myself, either during my childhood or before my birth. Why did You allow me to fall into error? Where were You and Your angels to rescue me? Perhaps You desire my conviction and that of others, or perhaps You only save those whom You love and choose?"

Then, He took me on a journey into the past. In the beginning, I learned about the mystery of good and bad hearts and why some were saved while others were condemned. I discovered that the truth had been concealed from humanity due to convenience and fear. They believed it was convenient to guide them only as far as was necessary for their sanctification.

I witnessed spirits that passed into the realm of death and emerged possessing wisdom (knowledge of good and evil). They attempted to testify to what they had seen. There were also those who practiced crossing the boundary between life and death, purifying themselves beforehand to avoid death. This practice had been observed by holy men since ancient times.

I saw the unworthy ones who touched the threshold of death, those who used drugs. When in a drugged state, they entered and communed with demons because, in that altered state, they carried the essence of impurity within them. The demons detested these carnal essences for having invaded their territory, and the demons claimed ownership of these individuals from that moment on. The days of these individuals were numbered.

Escaping was difficult because their spiritual essences were like incense to the demons, who delighted in this impurity. It served as a complete offering for the demons from the very beginning. All benevolent spirits that had once protected these individuals and all sanctifying grace departed from them. They were left alone and confused, unable to discern what was good. They found themselves in the world, perturbed and contributing to the empire of evil.

They were then delivered to commit clumsiness of all sorts, descending further into impurity to the point of seeking it desperately. As a last resort, they were granted over to the demons. If they couldn't find reconciliation through God's mercy, mediated by Jesus and the sacramental order of His church, all impure acts were marked by the demons with indignation. This was to deter them from approaching the Holy Church and seeking salvation, ultimately pushing them toward condemnation.

The cause of their fear of presenting themselves before God was their stain, which was sin. I observed how the demon twisted God's love, which was originally piety and courage in His service, into something else—an incorrect dignity, a hollow and meaningless form of dignity: pride, arrogance, haughtiness, and aggression.

Then, I asked God: "Lord, at what moment did I stain my heart without realizing it? When did I become deserving of Your contempt, and why didn't I perceive it, if only I had received a sign?"

He took me back to my adolescence when I didn't fully comprehend the Gospel. He took me to the moment when my heart couldn't bear humiliation. During a period of desperation, I succumbed to hatred, and at that moment, I heard my thoughts as clearly as He heard them from His throne. Impelled by fury, I made an oath that was recorded in all my being by the intensity for which I wished it. At that moment, His protective light turned away from me because of my hatred. He does not dwell among those who harbor hatred, as hatred is not of Him. I came to understand that, with my attitude, I had been increasingly driving His presence away.

I had nothing more to say. I realized that I had not lived for the sake of physical health or youth up to that moment. Throughout all this time, I had lived by God's mercy because God had already set a time for me to give an account of myself. I also understood that nobody had the right to despise a soul, for nobody is the owner of even the soul they possess. It is a grave offense against God to despise the spirit through acts like suicide. In such cases, the physical parents bear responsibility for the loss of the spirit because they failed to impart the teachings of the Gospel and God's knowledge, failing to provide the meaning of existence and an appreciation for the wonders of the Creator, God.

I felt great fear for my family, so I prayed to the Lord for my parents and grandparents, who are still alive. I pleaded with Him that in case I condemned myself, at least they would be saved.

God showed me how my mother's innocence adorned her like a crown, despite being a mother. In her heart, a radiant red glow, like that of a Ruby, shone, and thus, it held great value before God. Her heart was filled with a fervent devotion to morality and God's love, and I saw that my father would soon be sanctified in his spirit through her perseverance and bravery.

I also saw that God's call would come to each of my brothers at some point in their lives, and they would find their vocations. All of this was due to the tireless prayers and intercession offered by my maternal grandparents with their purity and dedication. God always listened to and granted their petitions because of their unwavering faithfulness.

I could no longer bear asking Him more questions. He possessed answers to all inquiries, all conveyed through selfexplanatory images! I felt as though my very being was on the verge of exploding. The images were rushing by at an incredible speed, yet I managed to grasp every detail, all of which seemed to contribute against me.

My pains and torments intensified as I realized that there was no salvation for me. With the profound anguish in my soul, I completely surrendered to His will, and finally, I asked Him, "Tell me, Lord, what will become of my child? Perhaps he will come to know You and be saved?"

He once again revealed to me through images that my son would experience moments of incomprehension and rebellion, getting lost for a time during his adolescence, and then ultimately being claimed by God. (My son had a unique destiny as he had been brought back to both physical and spiritual life; when he was four months old, he teetered between life and death but returned to life precisely during his baptism).

I felt profound sadness at the thought of the suffering my death would cause him, and I implored God for an opportunity. I asked

Him to return me to life because I longed to witness my son's growth. I knew that I was all he had in the world, and no one else could care for and guide him with a mother's love and devotion.

Then, the decisive moment arrived, and I was overwhelmed with fear at the thought of hearing His condemnation. I would have rather died a thousand times than hear that word which would condemn me to the terrible and tormenting place I had already glimpsed. I would have preferred to disappear with the pain of never having existed rather than face that fate, but there was no punishment more just than that for offending God.

I was consumed by desperation at the prospect of losing God's presence forever, so I clung to memories of Him. I thought of the countryside with all its wonders—the light and warmth of the sun, the waters, the animals, and the reflection of God's face in every human being I had encountered in life. I tried to carry all those memories with me for the moment of condemnation. However, what distressed me even more was that I had not known God in all His creations.

My torment became even more unbearable when I saw creation as He sees it. Everything in existence was honoring Him; all the animals perceived His presence and acknowledged His existence. Their only fear was the possibility of offending Him, and they obeyed His will in all things. The grasses offered Him the aroma and beauty of their flowers in their fullest splendor. The entire universe was surrendered to God's will; nothing moved without His authorization, and it presented itself to God as an infinite spectacle, for God's spirit was within everything, and this presence was referred to as Wisdom. God knew everything, and He was omnipresent. God did not lose any of His power even as His Wisdom expanded throughout creation.

This brought me profound sadness because the creation that He loved the most didn't know Him, and some even denied His existence. In desperation, I pleaded for forgiveness on behalf of the entire world. However, I felt that my supplication was no longer worth it, as it was already too late for me, and in my earthly life, I had also not known Him as I did at that moment. I was overwhelmed with regret for having wasted both my time and His. I recalled the purpose for which I was born and the promise I had made not to forget Him, and I realized that I had failed Him. I had indulged in worldly matters and lost my way.

The demons remained there, attentive and watchful, with their brilliant eyes gleaming with fury and impurity, reflecting contempt, and eagerly awaiting my fate.

The large demon, demanding and waiting for me, exuded anxiety, pride, and arrogance. He was convinced that God would deliver me into his hands, and he, too, awaited the final word.

Then, God showed me some people I had encountered in life, as well as others whom I had not known, and He asked me, "What do you think I should do with these people and their attitudes towards you?"

Confused, I responded: "Lord, these people haven't offended me. Why do You say it's against me?"

He then showed me images of situations where I had clashed with them to the point of pushing me to my limits. I said to Him, "Lord, please do not take into account what these people have done against me. Instead, guide them to get to know You. As for me, I only ask that You help me not to harbor hatred or resentment in my heart, so my soul remains unstained."

Still puzzled, I inquired, "Lord, why do You torment me with something that wasn't or will never be?"

He replied, "Because I want to see how you will handle them."

At that instant, a light separated from the radiance of God and sped towards me with astonishing speed. Before I could react, it passed through my being. For a brief moment, I feared it would condemn me, but instead, this light filled me with life, and all my suffering vanished. I was profoundly impressed because this light was contrary to everything I had previously experienced. It retook me to see the moment in my present life!

In that moment, my physical body lay motionless in the hospital bed with the last glimmer in my eyes! The doctors were around me waiting for any sign of reaction or my death, as there was nothing more they could do!

I saw my spirit suspended, positioned at the upper right side of my body, held on to my head, and in front of me, I had Felix contemplating my face! I thought the light had brought me to my final opportunity to witness my spirit separating from my body before condemnation.

In this image that I was contemplating from Felix and doctors, the light took me to the body of a crucified man experiencing death with the same agony of feeling how his spirit was separating from his pure body and spirit, unblemished by any offense, even against himself. He possessed a steadfast determination to fulfill the divine command and mission always revealed to him by God. I saw him experiencing and entering the realm of death, but he wasn't getting covered with the shadow, nor was death coming for him. Instead, It was death in total that was submitted to him because it was a necessity for him to enter it, fully aware that he had to experience the same death every human being would undergo while in a physical body.

After revealing all this and allowing me to feel what he felt during his agony, he noticed another man gazing at him, witnessing his crucifixion. The observer pondered, "Could this man truly be God's son? Even if he isn't, he certainly doesn't deserve what he's enduring." This observer was overcome with repentance, moved by a deep sense of sorrow for the crucified man.

Then, the man dying on the cross thought: "For men like you, it is worth dying, if only they would have compassion for one another."

Afterward, that image transformed into a man with a living essence. It was almost unbelievable; he had a corporeal essence and spirit, and I perceived his presence through his purity in this spiritual dimension. His essence carried a scent like that of a month-old baby and yet, it was also distinctly masculine, emitting a delightful aroma. He resembled a soothing breeze that provided inner satisfaction, much like the freshness and purity of water. A being descended from heaven, breaking free from the radiance of God, and passed through death to reach me. He filled me with life, peace, and light. Everything unfolded so quickly. His voice resonated splendidly within my soul, and his presence exuded purity and authority.

He spoke to me while gazing at Felix, who was contemplating my face: "I too had a compassionate one."

In that moment, I knew without a doubt that this extraordinary man was Jesus. Out of curiosity, I yearned to understand what He had done to relieve me of my torments. So, I turned my focus inward, and I saw that He was embracing and covering my nakedness and sins with His white garment, purifying me, and healing my spirit. At that point, my thirst was quenched. I could never forget what resided within Him, nor could I adequately describe it; it was akin to perfect happiness.

Jesus conveyed to me, "You are not destined for heaven, nor are you to be condemned. Remember why you were born."

I began to recollect a dream I had once. In that dream, I found myself in heaven, desiring to be born. However, as I walked through the Earth and witnessed its desolation, I yearned to return to heaven, but I couldn't find my way back. God told me, "No one can cross the line of life and return emptyhanded; one must fulfill their purpose." In response to my prayers, God had granted me a spirit to help me discover my purpose and ultimately return to Him. I had also made a promise to God that I would never forget Him.

Then, I looked at Felix, and I couldn't believe it; it was him! In the dream, the spirit had led me to the entrance of a cave and told me that my purpose could be found there, in the devil's house. I had to confront and defeat the devil to obtain it, because he was guarding it. The spirit had explained that he couldn't accompany me because purposes are personal, and he would wait for me until I emerged. In the dream, I had been fearful and had asked him with doubt why he was so sure I would triumph and return. His response was filled with unwavering confidence: "You will return, and I'll be here waiting for you."

I was struck by the realization that what I had always thought was just a dream had become my reality. This dream had lingered in my mind, yet I hadn't understood its significance until now. I realized that the devil's house represented death, and I had to confront death itself. The spirit waiting outside death was Felix. Now, I understood why he couldn't accompany me. My confrontation was personal, but I still didn't know if I had succeeded or if I would emerge victoriously.

At that moment, Jesus was imparting an overwhelming sense of peace and infusing my spirit with life. It was an indescribable sensation, one I had never encountered before, and I doubted its existence in this world. I can only express that I was utterly captivated by His presence and His voice, which I wished would never cease. If He had granted me the opportunity to go with Him, I would have left everything behind without hesitation.

I listened attentively and with great sensitivity to Jesus, the pure man with the essence of life. He conveyed to me, "You will fulfill your purpose, and you will present it, or you will face eternal condemnation. In the Father's house, individuals are known by their merits in their deeds, and for having abandoned your own, you cannot ascend."

I asked Him, "How can I fulfill my purpose if it already seems too late, and I'm determined not to face condemnation?"

He asked me, "Do you want to fulfill it, knowing everything there is in the world and facing what you already know, including evil, and overcoming your temptations?"

It was a difficult choice, but I realized that I didn't want to be condemned, as there appeared to be no way to avoid it. While I gazed at Him, I wondered, "What will He do to enable me to comply?" When I finally made my decision, I thought, "Yes, I do want to..." I hadn't even finished uttering the phrase when He swiftly returned me to my body. As I emerged from the verge of death, the demons remained in a state of reverence, their heads bowed, listening to the entire conversation. Once they saw that I was returning to life, they appeared surprised but did not protest. Amidst this, I managed to hear Jesus say to me, "Go, for everything is already arranged for you to fulfill it. You only need to comply with the things that correspond to you".

MY PURPOSE

My spirit settled into my body with an overwheling sense of joy and harmony. For the first time, I felt entirely at peace and free from moral and spiritual pain. However, I also experienced an intense physical thirst. My body was exhausted, frail, and deteriorated from the extensive medication and the muscle contractions endured during the agony. It was a physical thirst, as my spiritual thirst had been eternally satisfied by the mercy of Jesus Christ.

As I began to perceive all of this, I continued to hear Felix's words. He was pleading with them to provide me with water, but they declined, asserting that I wouldn't be able to consume it given my condition. Undeterred, Felix then requested that, if I couldn't drink water, they at least moisten my lips. He expressed concern as he noticed that my lips' skin had dried and adhered to my jawbones. In response, one of the nurses fetched a container of water, and Felix asked for something to apply it. The nurse offered him a piece of cotton gauze, which he moistened and gently applied to my parched lips. In that moment, I experienced a profound sensation of my spirit stirring with animation as it absorbed the moisture, despite the recent death experience I had just undergone. It was an extraordinary feeling that left me in awe, as I could distinctly feel my spirit moving within my body in response to the moisture from the water. It served as yet another confirmation that everything I had experienced was undeniably real. Subsequently, my brain detected the moisture and distributed it throughout my entire being, as if it were a magical elixir revitalizing all my impulses. It began with my nerves and culminated in the revitalization of my bones.

Finally, I found the strength to move, and I turned towards Felix. I was eager to express my gratitude and share everything I had experienced, seen, and heard. I wanted to convey to him why I was still alive and how God's compassion, combined with his actions, had contributed to my recovery. Moreover, I wished to tell him that Jesus had chosen him long before to assist me in fulfilling my sense of purpose and reveal the truth he had longed for - the knowledge of whether there is life beyond this one.

I yearned to jump and scream with joy because I was alive in body, spiritually conscious, and possessed knowledge of the profound mysteries behind God's creation. I felt incredibly fortunate. However, all I could manage was to touch Felix's hand as he began to withdraw it. I offered him a grateful smile, as my body was too exhausted to do more. Despite my physical limitations, I summoned all my remaining strength to speak. It was a struggle, and I even felt my throat strain as I spoke. With great effort, I told him that I was going to sleep because sleep was finally beckoning me.

It felt like a yearning for the body's renewal and the soul's repose, and I had no fear of surrendering to it. I was utterly drained, and this experience was the most demanding task I had ever faced in my life, incomparable to any other effort.

Though I remained completely conscious, retaining vivid memories of my life, my journey through the dimension of death, and my surroundings, I reassured Felix. I told him, "You can go home and rest now. I am sleepy, and I need to sleep." Upon hearing this, the doctors displayed visible concern, their expressions reflecting their worries. I overheard them mentioning the possibility that I might not wake up if I fell asleep. Felix shared their apprehension, so I added with conviction, "I won't die again. I'm just tired and in need of rest." I looked into his eyes to convey my assurance, and he sensed my newfound peace and improvement.

My body surrendered to sleep, and I could rest with the comforting assurance that everything was behind me. There would be plenty of time to share this remarkable experience! As I drifted into slumber, I reveled in the essence Jesus had left me—the essence of life in all its profound richness. It felt akin to a rebirth, enveloping me in absolute peace devoid of sadness, anger, or regret.

I awoke the following evening, still feeling as if I had been newly born. I sensed a profound lightness and inner tranquility, along with a renewed sense of potential.

I wanted to analyze all that I had done before this experience. Plus, that it was in my hands to fight against my customs and habits. I am now a new being internally, although nobody could notice it outwardly. And better yet, I had the knowledge of my sense of existence. I realized that God had attempted to reveal it to me in the past, but I didn't understand it. I thought that they had been coincidences, and my dreams of revelation had been just that, dreams, useless dreams, even came to believe that they were stupidities, a product of my imagination.

I felt an immense sense of gratitude for being alive, and I recognized the necessity of this profound experience. I endured unimaginable suffering, but I believed it was worthwhile, and I thanked God for it. Nonetheless, I had no desire to relive such an ordeal. I held firm in my faith that I would not have to go through something like this again because I had confidence that Jesus would protect me from another such experience. He had promised to take me to the house of His Father next time, and all I had to do was trust Him, wait patiently, and obey His guidance.

For the moment, my primary focus was on my physical recovery. The medications had deeply impacted my body, throwing off my immune system and natural bodily functions to the point where it had started shutting down. Given that my body had nearly succumbed to death, I needed to regain my strength, detoxify it from all the harmful substances, and allow it to reestablish its equilibrium. I wasn't certain how long this process would take, but I had faith that I would ultimately recover fully.

A young college student who dedicated her time to volunteering at the hospital, assisting the sick, greeted me and introduced herself. She ordered food for me and then attempted to feed me, which made me laugh. I told her I didn't need assistance because I already felt well. To prove it, I got out of bed and asked her to show me where the bathroom was so I could wash my hands. Upon returning, I sat at the edge of the bed to eat my meal. While I was calmly eating, she asked me, 'Why did you want to commit suicide? I don't understand why you reached the point of risking your life. If it weren't for the doctors who saved you, you might not have survived.

I thought it was a joke and started laughing with difficulty because I felt a lot of pain, especially in my abdomen. After all, it was fragile.

She looked at me, surprised, and said, 'How can you laugh? You attempted to take your own life. I understand that people have many problems, but you, you're laughing!'

Upon realizing the seriousness and absurdity of her comments, I became concerned and told her, 'If you prefer, we can discuss other topics, but please don't joke about this.

She said: "It is not a joke. One of the nurses said that you wanted to commit suicide by taking a bottle of pills, and she wrote it in your report ".

I couldn't believe it; discouragement overwhelmed me, and my motivation plummeted to the point where I couldn't speak. When I finally regained my composure, I said to the young college student, 'I didn't want to take my own life. That is something very serious, especially for me, as I am Catholic by heritage. It was an accident. Yes, I took some pills, but not with the intention of ending my life. I have many reasons to keep living. If I were to tell you all of them, we would never finish. I'll just say that I have a family to support, and I wouldn't want to bring them sorrow, especially in this way. Besides, the world is filled with beautiful things that I still want to experience.'

She added, 'The nurse also issued an order that no one should provide you with any objects or items with which you could attempt to harm yourself again.

In my conscience, I knew, and I was sure that I never wanted to take my life. That is something I would never do, and not even when I was suffering from my illness would I have thought of suicide. I endured the pain and frustration until the last moment, and now she informs me that they wrote my medical report as a case of suicide! The only thing I could do was pray in thought and ask the Lord with all my heart to take care of everything. Therefore, after I calmed down, I finished eating.

In my mind, a great sense of humiliation remained, knowing that this nurse dared to commit such an act behind my back without finding out or asking me first, while I was defenseless, delicate, and physically limited. I think it wouldn't have cost her much effort to find out, as I was in the hospital with them. It was a violation of my rights and dignity. I only asked the Lord to make her reflect because if she was accusing me of madness, what she had committed could be called much worse. In part, I understood because those who do not believe in God often equate humans and animals.

After a few hours, the phone rang. I was surprised because I wasn't expecting anyone. The young woman answered and said that it was for me. It was a nurse who asked if I wanted to receive a visitor. Curious about whom it might be, I accepted because I thought that it was the staff responsible for collecting patient information for the medical expenses.

Several minutes after the call, I saw that Felix was the one coming to see me. He was the last person I would have thought to visit me. And I don't blame him because I thought that maybe this experience had been too intense for him after seeing me suffer and agonize. Seeing him in front of me once more only confirmed to me what I had observed: the luminosity of his spirit when I was in front of him at the time I was experiencing death. Although he still didn't know what I had just been through, in my thoughts, he acted by himself, not motivated by any apparent reason or interest. A smile broke out on my face upon seeing him because he witnessed that I had known what death is. He was the sign that everything would be fulfilled to achieve my purpose, my sense of existence.

Felix is the other person that God had chosen so that our purpose could be fulfilled – giving testimony of God's existence and His constant interaction with us, humanity, and contributing to help anyone in the danger that I was, in both spiritual and physical death. And it was worth waiting for him until the time would finally come when I could confess to him that there is another life after this one.

After all of this, I found peace. I knew that the bar was the right place where I had to be to see for myself and understand everything that corrupts the spirits and offends God, including how one falls into the unconsciousness of impurity and many more things that have already been written in the previous pages of this book. And here I was, someone who had asked God many times to be relieved from this job!"

After a few months, everything we needed to fulfill our purpose started to come from God, beginning with a dream in which He asked me to rescue His people, much like in the times of Egypt. I replied, expressing my confusion because there is no slavery in today's world.

He responded: "From what enslaves them, from sin, the very reason for which they had to leave the land of Egypt. In Egypt, impurity was prevalent, much like it is today, and I don't want them to drift further from Me.

I humbly told Him: 'I may not be worthy due to my struggles with indignation, but if You will it, cleanse me and provide me with what I need.'

My indignation stemmed from the overwhelming anxiety caused by medication withdrawal. In an attempt to alleviate this anxiety, I had experimented with cigarettes and alcohol, but these efforts only pushed me deeper into impurity."

After leaving the hospital, I was once again prescribed medication, this time under pressure and threats that if I attempted to stop taking it, I would die, and even trying would lead to legal trouble. Despite these threats, I chose not to take the medication.

The fear of the claiming of God made me reflect. And once again, I surrendered to His mercy since I already knew of His infinite power because if He had granted me life again, it had also become clear to me that for Him, nothing is impossible.

Thereafter, everything started to happen. I finally dared to confess everything to Felix, and we concluded to make the book in the way of testimony. We weren't even finishing talking about it, and everything started to arrive in a convenient way that surprised me. Felix couldn't believe it, he witnessed it, and they even gave him the information we needed to publish a book.

To Felix's surprise, the man who gave him the information worked as a security guard at Felix's bar. He had just published a book about his own life, and on that particular day, he had a copy of it in his possession. Furthermore, he didn't speak Spanish, nor did I speak English for Felix to know that I couldn't have planned this encounter. Almost all the money we needed for the project came from tips, which was unusual as Felix had rarely received tips before. We used this money to purchase the necessary materials and began working on our project, which became our purpose. Felix understood that everything was coming from God.

Felix expresses his gratitude to God because he alone can truly comprehend the profound nature of these events and recognize that they are ultimately for the greater good and, most importantly, for God Himself. The purpose of our project is to assist those who seek to find meaning in their existence. Life is not merely a series of extraordinary coincidences; even in physical death, it marks the beginning of something new and eternal.

Félix A. Gomez

Felix's awakening began when I suggested writing a book. Intrigued by the book's subject matter, he inquired about the foundation of our writing venture. In response, I revealed my near-death experience, emphasizing that belief in my testimony wasn't necessary because, during my journey into death, I had witnessed that these revelations were already present in the Holy Bible.

Motivated by curiosity, Felix delved into the Bible himself, gradually uncovering the profound significance of my testimony. As he immersed himself in Scripture, he discovered his sense of existence and understood something that had caused him great frustration in his life: a conflict with one of his relatives and how the differences of personality turned them against each other. And being that the individual is his relative, he was determined not to inflict harm on his family member. However, the mounting frustration pushed him to his breaking point. Rather than committing a misfortune, he clamored to God, fervently praying and making a solemn promise to offer something special to the divine. He beseeched God to intervene, allowing him to disentangle himself from the problematic business they were embroiled in.

The critical distinction here is that Felix's relative had exploited Felix's good credit to secure the business he desired. Furthermore, without seeking consent, he utilized Felix's credit for personal expenses, charging them to the business's account, which was also under Felix's name.

Felix's desperation intensified when he discovered his relative's covert activities, which included practices like offerings and concealed amulets, akin to "witchcraft," all designed to provoke and disturb Felix. In response, Felix sought to extricate himself from the business. He attempted to sell half of the business, which belonged to him, to another individual in an effort to disentangle himself. However, his relative vehemently opposed this proposition and among others, as well as rejecting Felix's peaceable overtures. Consequently, Felix initiated a legal process, and after numerous legal proceedings, he eventually managed to sever his ties with the business through a negotiated settlement.

Two months later, he traveled to Santiago, Dominican Republic, and fulfilled the offering he had promised to God. He said that During this act of fulfillment, the people who received it gave him their blessing. This experience left him feeling profoundly blessed, emotionally moved, and worthy to ask God for more. He prayed to be used for God's service, to receive wisdom for a deeper understanding of God, and to reveal the purpose and meaning of his existence.

During several months, he was incapacitated because of the frustration and damages that caused him to associate with his relative. Additionally, he was disheartened by the disillusionment he acquired from the numerous customers who frequented the business and observed everything happening within its walls. This experience led him to make a solemn vow never to involve himself in this type of business again.

Eight months later, a friend paid him a visit and persistently urged him to consider a business that was up for sale. Despite Felix's prior reservations due to his previous experiences, his friend's unwavering insistence led him to explore the opportunity that lay before him. Through his friend's encouragement, the confidence gained from his past experiences, and the straightforwardness of the procedures involved, Felix sensed that this opportunity was meant for him, a divine calling from God. Consequently, he became the owner of this establishment, and during the initial two years of ownership, he prospered. In gratitude, he attributed his success to God, viewing it as a reward for his patient faith and unwavering prayers.

I observed that Felix harbored significant resentment whenever he recollected his interactions with his relative. However, as he delved into the Holy Bible to verify my testimony, a transformation occurred within him. He began to find solace and understanding within the scriptures, gradually letting go of his bitterness.

Felix came to the realization that harboring resentment and hatred went against God's teachings and was, therefore, unacceptable. This newfound understanding led Felix to a profound conclusion; he wanted the book to be written. He desired to share with others how his journey to know God had liberated him, especially those who needed it most. In this revelation, he understood that the reward of patiently waiting on God with unwavering faith was not measured in material wealth but in spiritual growth and fulfillment.

Maria R. Mendoza

Thank God for granting me the opportunity to share this testimony with all of you. My heartfelt prayer is for God to awaken your spirits and lead each one of us towards the eternal light.

POEMS
The Tomb

The tomb: It's more than a resting place for the body, beyond a spot where dear ones recall your name.

It's a personal mansion, heaven's gift – a blanket of stars, soothing breezes, and warm embrace.

The ground serves as your bed, but it's more than mere earth. It witnessed your growth, first steps, playful days, and tumbles, and when you fell, while you cried from the scrape, it would take advantage to give you a caress.

It endured with pain your cultivation, edifications, and your machinery.

In moments of sadness or boredom, it silently shared the fragrance of its flowers, the colors of its fields and waters, the marvels of its creatures. All this, in anticipation of the day it could cradle you in its arms, showering you with kisses.

Above you, on top of where you'll rest eternally, an adorned tombstone, a testament to your existence, will endure in accordance with your deeds. It stands as your timeless sanctuary.

Life Without God Is A Dream

You dream that you are, that you possess, that you love, and that they love you. You dream that you yearn, that you aspire, and that you ultimately achieve. A dream from which, at any moment, one can awaken and realize that you have ceased to exist, no longer possess anything, that they didn't love you eternally as they once vowed. You didn't love eternally as you reiterated time and time again. That nothing ever truly belonged to you, and you never truly belonged to anyone, not even to yourself...

"I"

The power to do good always resided within me. The capacity for evil also dwelled within me, and it was called "I."

"I" was capable of good because it existed within me.

"I" was also capable of evil because it stirred within me, and everyone saw that it was "I."

Some said, "She's such a good girl," while others remarked, "That little girl can be so wicked!" It didn't bother me because I didn't fully comprehend; all I knew was that it was "I."

During that time, I had no knowledge of heaven or hell, but suddenly, I found myself between the two.

I realized that if I ended up in hell, it would be "I" who would be there because only "I" mattered.

And if I were destined for heaven, it was because of my capacity for love, my willingness to let others find happiness, even if it meant sacrificing myself. In the end, it was "I" who determined my path, deciding what to do, what not to do, and where to go, for ultimately, "I" would be there.

The Church

Be grateful to God for the Church, which provides us with order in our lives through its commandments. We are also thankful for the teachings it imparts, allowing us to share the knowledge of God's love with others. Through this, we come together as one family, the family of God!

The Desire Of My Heart

I yearned for the riches of this world, and the demon wasted no time. Swift as a flash, he stood before me, offering his contract to grant me the world and place it at my feet. He tried to persuade me with honeyed words, saying, "It's what you need to find happiness, and there's no harm in seeking happiness!" He presented himself impeccably from head to toe and repeated his enticing words again and again. Finally, seeking to absolve himself of responsibility before God and leaving me as the sole culprit in the eyes of both God and my fellow beings, he pretended to rob me, even leaving me stripped of my dignity, to roam in humiliation. With a sinister grin, he said, "If you wish, I won't force you!"

My Heart Seeks The Light

My heart is in constant longing; it resides in a state of anxious fear. It trembles as though it has a premonition of its own demise when it strays from Your presence, God the Father. It fears losing Your love, and it cannot find solace until You bestow upon it Your eternal peace. I am aware that this yearning will persist until the moment I gaze upon the radiant brilliance of Your countenance, Your light, and Your glory.

J. Soledad. Reynoso. Garza.

The garden of the peace: I find my lullaby in the murmurs of your songs, surrounded by the fragrance of flowers in your gentle embrace, and enveloped in the soothing comfort you provide. Loneliness is an infinite void, much like your memory, to which I cling tightly, preventing myself from falling into the abyss of the world. It serves as my lifeline.

You shall forever reign in my heart, spanning from generation to generation, and your name will always be held in the highest regard, just as it was when I used to watch you pass by. My lady, I implore you to reserve a place for me in your heart and mind, so that when you pray, your prayers may encompass me as well. Through your intercession, I find the means to live.

In The Adolescence

God communicates in the silence of our actions, in the hushed tones of love, in the quiet depths of our essence, and in the unspoken language of our emotions.

God's voice can be heard as a gentle melody in the silence of slumber, in the tranquil movements of the clouds. He expresses His love and gently whispers to our hearts through intuition.

He beckons, "If you desire to know more, come, walk with me, and you shall witness the beauty of my Kingdom.

FAREWELLS

Maria R. Mendoza

I express my heartfelt gratitude to my grandparents, Mr. and Mrs. Felipe Matamoros Gonzales and Soledad Reinoso Garza, for their unwavering prayers on behalf of us, their descendants. They have imparted to me the invaluable teachings about the knowledge of God.

I am deeply thankful to my parents, Angel and Gero Mendoza, for the gift of life and the privilege of growing up with my beloved siblings: Ever, Ana, Miguel, Luis, and Juan.

My sincere appreciation extends to our godparents, Eugenio and Icnasia Cervantes, and to Mr. Fabián Ortiz, his wife, and their family. They have been like second parents to my brothers and me, offering us unwavering support and invaluable guidance in our understanding of God's doctrine.

I offer my gratitude to God for the presence of Felix A. Gomez in my life, for his support and understanding during the most critical moments.

Thanks be to God for the creation, for His infinite compassion, and His constant intervention. I am grateful for the sacrifice of Jesus, the Son of God, and His Holy Mother, Mary, who is also the mother of all saints, the Pope, bishops, priests, deacons, laymen, Catholic religious orders, and more.

My wish is for God to awaken your spirits and bestow a life filled with blessings. May He strengthen you to resist temptation and guide you towards His Kingdom.

Sending warm greetings to my spiritual brother, "Rami"!

Félix A. Gomez

I wish to express my deepest gratitude to my grandparents, Mr. and Mrs. Teofido De Jesus Gomez Márquez and Luz Eduvina Gomez Ascona, who now rest in the eternal glory of God. They imparted invaluable lessons of faith and patience in waiting on God. I also extend my thanks to God for my entire family.

I am immensely grateful to God for allowing me to be a part of this project, for granting me the wisdom to deepen my knowledge of Him, for bestowing upon me a sense of existence, and for enabling me to contribute alongside Maria R. Mendoza to your spiritual awakening.

Both Felix A. Gomez and Maria R. Mendoza extend our heartfelt thanks to the following gentlemen:

- Bernardo Figueroa

- Tim Goldy Williams

- David A. Hendler, our lawyer

We appreciate your humility and your invaluable assistance during the moments when we needed it most.

WITH COURTESY

The comprehension and knowledge of the writings in this book begin to develop from our personal experiences with God. Our aim is to provide an understanding of the testimony that there indeed exists another life after this one and that there is a creator of everything.

The practice of Catholicism goes beyond mere rituals and beliefs. It extends to the deep recognition of the living God, even in the absence of complete comprehension or direct sight. "It is a personal affirmation of faith", a spiritual connection that transcends the mere inscription of the Holy Bible or individual interpretations and inspirations.

www.ingramcontent.com/pod-product-compliance
Lightning Source LLC
Chambersburg PA
CBHW070729160426
43192CB00009B/1365